Kitchen Treasury Series

POULTRY

Editorial Director
   DONALD D. WOLF

Design and Layout
   MARGOT L. WOLF

Published by
LEXICON PUBLICATIONS, INC.
387 Park Avenue South, New York, NY 10016

Cover illustration:
Game Hens with Spicy Stuffing, 48

Opposite title page:
Bouillon Coq, 23

Copyright © 1987 by
Advance Publishers
1146 Solana Avenue
Winter Park, Florida 32789

ISBN: 0-7172-4519-5

Contents

Introduction, 7
Chicken, 9
Rock Cornish Hens, 48
Turkeys, 51
Ducklings, 59
Geese, 65
Squabs, Pigeons, and Game Birds, 67
Sauces and Side Dishes, 74
Index, 79

Introduction

Poultry includes all domesticated birds used for food: chicken (including capon), turkey, goose, duckling, guinea and squab. Recently the Rock-Cornish game hen, a delicious hybrid, has been added. Wild duck and pheasant are game birds which are handled like domestic poultry. Rabbit, either domestic or wild, has meat so similar to poultry that it is included here.

CLASSES—Chickens and turkeys are classified according to size, age and sex. Age influences tenderness of the meat and therefore determines the cooking method. Size determines the cooking time.

Chicken—*Broiler,* either sex, 1½ to 2½ lbs. ready-to-cook weight, 10 to 12 weeks old; *fryer,* either sex, 2 to 3 lbs. ready-to-cook weight, 12 to 16 weeks old; *roaster,* either sex, usually over 3½ lbs., usually under 8 months; *capon,* unsexed male, usually under 10 months, 4 lbs. or over, exceptionally good flavor, especially tender, with large proportion of white meat; *stewing chicken,* female, usually more than 10 months, 3 to 5 lbs. ready-to-cook weight.

Turkey—*Fryer-roaster,* either sex, usually under 16 weeks, 4 to 8 lbs. ready-to-cook weight; *young hen or tom,* female or male, usually under 8 months, 8 to 24 lbs. ready-to-cook weight; *mature hen or tom,* over 10 months, less tender and seldom found on the consumer market.

Duck—*Duckling,* either sex, 8 to 9 weeks old, 3½ to 5 lbs. ready-to-cook weight (the only class in which ducks are marketed commercially).

Goose—Classifications less well established, but weights range from 4 to 8 lbs. ready-to-cook weight for young birds, up to 14 lbs. for mature birds.

STYLES—*Dressed poultry* refers to birds which have been bled and feather-dressed but have head, feet and viscera intact. *Ready-to-cook poultry* is fully cleaned inside and out and is ready for cooking; it may or may not be tagged or stamped with official inspection or grade labels. (Since 1953, only ready-to-cook poultry is permitted to carry United States Department of Agriculture grades on individual birds; but the use of official inspection and grading services is entirely voluntary on the part of the packers.) Ready-to-cook poultry is marketed either fresh, ice-chilled or quick-frozen. In many markets, chicken and turkey halves, quarters, pieces and giblets are sold separately, fresh or quick-frozen. These pieces—especially breast, thighs and drumsticks—greatly simplify cooking and serving poultry and facilitate meal-planning. Quick-frozen *stuffed* turkeys must be cooked without thawing. DO NOT FREEZE YOUR OWN STUFFED TURKEY as the time required to freeze them with stuffing encourages the growth of bacteria.

BUYING GUIDES—Where tags or stamps provide information as to quality established by inspection and grading or both, this is the consumer's most reliable guide in the selection of poultry. The grading and inspection program of the United States Department of Agriculture employs three easily recognizable marks: 1) *inspection mark,* indicating that the bird has been processed under sanitary conditions and is wholesome food; 2) *grade mark,* indicating the quality, class and kind—there are three grades, A, B and C; 3) *grade and inspection mark.* Poultry bearing the combined grade and inspection marks is guaranteed to be of top quality.

When grading and inspection labels are not present, the consumer may be guided by some of the standards used in official grading. Young birds have smooth, soft, thin skin, little fat and flexible-tipped breastbones; as the bird ages, the skin coarsens, more fat is deposited along the backbone and the breastbone becomes more rigid. Grade A quality requires that a bird be well-formed and full-fleshed, with no defects, tears or bruises in the skin, clean and free from pinfeathers.

STORAGE—Poultry is a perishable food and must be safeguarded against spoilage or deterioration of flavor by proper care. *Quick-frozen* poultry must be kept frozen until ready to use and once thawed must not be refrozen. In thawing frozen poultry before cooking, directions on the label should be followed. *Fresh or ice-chilled* poultry should be purchased only at markets where the birds are kept refrigerated. To store poultry of this style at home, remove it from the meat dealer's wrappings and rewrap it loosely; then store in the coldest part of the refrigerator (about 40°F). Cut-up poultry should be held no more than 24 hours before using; whole birds with the giblets wrapped separately may be stored up to two days.

PREPARATION FOR COOKING—*Ready-to-cook* poultry, whole or in pieces, should be rinsed in cold water, drained immediately and patted dry. It should never be allowed to soak in water, as soaking dissipates flavor. *Dressed* poultry should be drawn immediately, preferably at the market. Remove pinfeathers with a sharp-pointed knife or a strawberry huller. Singe the bird over a flame, turning quickly until all down and hair are burnt off. Then wash as for ready-to-cook poultry.

Before roasting, neck and body cavities of whole birds are rubbed with a mixture of salt and Accent, then usually stuffed (never stuff until ready to roast), trussed and roast-meat thermometer inserted. Poultry pieces generally are coated with a mixture of flour, salt, pepper, Accent and other seasonings if desired, before frying or browning; before broiling, they are seasoned with salt, pepper and Accent.

COAT POULTRY PIECES EVENLY—Put a mixture of flour and seasonings into a bowl or onto a piece of waxed paper. Coat one or a few pieces of poultry at a time. Or shake a few pieces at a time in a plastic or clean paper bag containing the flour mixture.

COOKING POULTRY—Two general principles apply to the cooking of all kinds of poultry: 1) Cook at low to moderate constant heat for a suitable length of time. High temperatures shrink the muscle tissue and make the meat tough, dry and hard. Poultry should always be cooked until well done; the meat should separate easily from the bone and should be tender to the fork. An exception is wild duck, which is traditionally served rare. 2) Suit the method of cooking to the age or class of the bird. Young birds of all kinds may be broiled, fried or roasted in an open pan. Older, less tender birds require cooking by moist heat, either in a covered casserole or Dutch oven, or in water or steam.

STUFFING POULTRY FOR ROASTING—Ingredients for a stuffing should be mixed *just before needed* and the bird should be stuffed *just before roasting*. Never stuff bird a day in advance and store in refrigerator or freezer. These are safety precautions to prevent food poisoning, since stuffing is the perfect medium for disease-producing bacteria. *Immediately* after the meal is served, remove the stuffing from the bird and store, covered, in the refrigerator. Use leftover stuffing within 2 or 3 days and heat thoroughly before serving.

Any extra stuffing which cannot be put into the bird may be put in a greased, covered baking dish or wrapped in aluminum foil and baked in the oven during the last hour of roasting.

TESTS FOR DONENESS OF ROAST POULTRY—A roast-meat thermometer, if used, should register 190° F when bird is done (insert in center of inside thigh muscle). The thickest part of drumstick feels soft when pressed with fingers protected with clean cloth or paper napkin. Or drumstick moves up and down or twists out of joint easily.

STORING COOKED POULTRY—Cooked poultry, gravy and stuffing should not be left at room temperature for longer than it takes to finish the meal. Never store bird with stuffing; remove stuffing and store it covered in refrigerator; cover gravy and refrigerate. If only one side of a roast bird has been carved, wrap remainder of bird in waxed paper, aluminum foil or moisture-vapor-proof material; store in refrigerator. If more than one half of the meat has been used, remove the remaining meat from the bones and wrap tightly before storing. Cooked pieces should be tightly wrapped and refrigerated. Do not keep cooked poultry, however carefully stored, for more than a few days.

Honey-Glazed Filbert Roast Chicken (page 9)

Chicken

Roast Chicken with Potatoes

5 SERVINGS

1 chicken (about 4 pounds)
Salt and pepper to taste
Juice of 1 lemon
¼ cup butter
¼ teaspoon paprika
1 cup water
5 medium potatoes, pared

1. Season chicken, inside and out, with salt, pepper, lemon juice, butter, and paprika. Place chicken on a rack in a baking dish.
2. Bake at 350°F about 1¼ hours, or until chicken is tender, basting occasionally. After the first 30 minutes of cooking, pour in water; add potatoes and baste with drippings.
3. Turn oven control to 400°F. Remove chicken to a platter and keep warm. Turn potatoes over in dish. Bake an additional 5 to 10 minutes.

Honey-Glazed Filbert Roast Chicken

6 SERVINGS

½ package herb-seasoned stuffing mix (2 cups)
1 cup toasted filberts, chopped
½ cup chopped celery
1 chicken liver, finely chopped
½ cup butter or margarine, melted
½ cup water
1 roaster-fryer or capon, about 5 pounds
½ cup honey
2 tablespoons soy sauce
1 teaspoon grated orange peel
2 tablespoons orange juice

1. Combine stuffing mix with the filberts, celery, chicken liver, butter, and water; toss lightly. Stuff cavity of chicken with the mixture, then tie chicken legs and wings with cord to hold close to body.
2. Place chicken, breast up, on rack in a shallow roasting pan. Roast at 325°F 2½ to 3 hours, or until chicken tests done. (The thickest part of drumstick feels soft when pressed with fingers and meat thermometer registers 180° to 185°F.)
3. Meanwhile, combine honey, soy sauce, and orange peel and juice. Brush chicken frequently with the mixture during last hour of roasting.

Roast Chicken with Orange-Beer Sauce

6 SERVINGS

1 roasting chicken (4 to 5 pounds)
Stuffing (optional)
Salt and pepper
1 can or bottle (12 ounces) beer
½ cup orange juice
2 tablespoons lemon juice
2 tablespoons tomato paste or ketchup
2 teaspoons sugar
¼ cup flour
Fresh parsley and orange slices

1. Stuff chicken, if desired; truss. Rub with salt and pepper. Place in a roasting pan.
2. Combine 1 cup beer, orange juice, lemon juice, tomato paste, and sugar. Pour a little over chicken.
3. Roast, uncovered, at 375°F 2 to 2½ hours, or until done, basting occasionally with remaining beer mixture.
4. Transfer chicken to platter; keep warm. Skim fat from drippings; measure remaining liquid. If needed, add water to make 1½ cups. Make paste with flour and remaining ½ cup beer. Combine with liquid. Cook, stirring constantly, until thickened. Season with salt and pepper to taste.
5. Garnish chicken with parsley and orange slices. Pass sauce to pour over slices after carving.

(continued)

Ham-Bread Stuffing for Chicken: Combine **3 cups fresh bread cubes, ¼ pound ground ham, 1 small onion, minced, 2 tablespoons melted butter, ½ teaspoon salt, ¼ teaspoon sage, a dash pepper,** and just enough **beer** to moisten.

Roast Chicken Tarragon

4 SERVINGS

1 broiler-fryer chicken (2½ to 3 pounds)
2 teaspoons clarified butter
2 teaspoons snipped fresh or 1 teaspoon dried tarragon leaves
Salt
2 carrots, cut in 1-inch pieces
1 small onion, cut in quarters
1 stalk celery, cut in 1-inch pieces
2 sprigs parsley
1¼ cups Chicken Stock (page 74)
1 tablespoon arrowroot
Cold water
½ teaspoon salt
¼ teaspoon freshly ground white pepper
2 teaspoons snipped fresh or 1 teaspoon dried tarragon leaves
2 tablespoons dry sherry

1. Rinse chicken; pat dry. Place in a roasting pan. Brush chicken with clarified butter; sprinkle with 2 teaspoons tarragon. Sprinkle cavity with salt; fill cavity with carrot, onion, celery, and parsley.
2. Roast in a 325°F oven about 2½ hours, or until chicken is done; meat on drumstick will be very tender. Remove chicken to a platter. Remove vegetables; reserve. Cover loosely with aluminum foil and let stand 20 minutes before carving.
3. Spoon fat from roasting pan. Heat stock to simmering in roasting pan, stirring to incorporate particles from pan. Mix arrowroot with a little cold water; stir into stock with salt, pepper, 2 teaspoons tarragon, and the sherry. Simmer, stirring constantly, until stock is thickened (about 5 minutes).
4. Slice chicken and arrange on platter. Garnish with reserved vegetables. Serve with sauce.

Pennsylvania Dutch Roast Chicken

4 TO 6
SERVINGS

1 roaster chicken, 3 to 4
  pounds
Butter or margarine,
  softened
Bread Stuffing
1 cup dairy sour cream

1. Rub inside of chicken with a mixture of **salt** and **pepper,** then rub generously with butter. Fill with stuffing; sew, or skewer and lace with cord.
2. Put chicken into a roasting pan; cover.
3. Roast at 400°F 1½ to 2 hours, or until chicken is tender; about every 15 minutes during roasting spoon some of the sour cream over the chicken. Remove cover for the last 30 minutes of roasting if a darker brown is desired.
4. For a thicker gravy, **1 tablespoon flour** may be stirred into the liquid in pan after removing the chicken. Set pan over heat and bring mixture to boiling, stirring constantly; boil 1 minute.

Bread Stuffing: Soak **4 slices white bread** in **cold water** and squeeze out all excess moisture. Using a fork, fluff bread and drizzle with **2 tablespoons melted butter or margarine.** Blend into **1 slightly beaten egg** a mixture of **1 teaspoon salt, ⅛ teaspoon black pepper,** and **¼ teaspoon poultry seasoning,** then **1 teaspoon chopped parsley** and **1 teaspoon grated onion.** Add egg mixture to bread mixture and toss lightly until thoroughly mixed. If desired, **finely chopped cooked giblets** may be added.

Stuffed Roast Capon

6 TO 8
SERVINGS

½ cup butter or margarine
1½ teaspoons salt
¼ teaspoon ground black
  pepper
¼ teaspoon thyme
¼ teaspoon marjoram
¼ teaspoon rosemary
1½ quarts soft enriched
  bread cubes
½ cup milk
¼ cup chopped celery leaves
¼ cup chopped onion
1 capon (6 to 7 pounds)
Salt
Fat, melted

1. For stuffing, melt butter and mix in salt, pepper, thyme, marjoram, and rosemary.
2. Put bread cubes into a large bowl and pour in seasoned butter; lightly toss. Mix in milk, celery leaves, and onion.
3. Rub body and neck cavities of capon with salt. Fill cavities lightly with stuffing; truss bird, using skewers and cord.
4. Place, breast side up, on rack in a shallow roasting pan. Brush skin with melted fat and cover with a fat-moistened cheesecloth.
5. Roast in a 325°F oven 2½ hours, or until a meat thermometer inserted in center of inside thigh muscle registers 180°F to 185°F. For easier carving, allow capon to stand about 20 minutes after removing from oven. Serve on a heated platter.

Capon Roasted in Salt

4 SERVINGS

1 capon (about 5 pounds)
Salt
1 carrot, cut in 1-inch pieces
1 medium onion, cut in
  quarters
2 sprigs parsley
6 to 7 pounds coarse kosher
  salt
Watercress

1. Rinse capon; pat dry. Salt inside of cavity lightly; fill cavity with vegetables.
2. Line a deep Dutch oven (that will fit size of capon, allowing 1½ to 2 inches space on bottom, sides, and top) with heavy-duty aluminum foil, allowing 2 inches of foil to fold down over top edge of pan. Fill bottom of Dutch oven with a 1½-inch layer of salt. Place capon in Dutch oven. Carefully fill Dutch oven with salt, being careful not to get salt inside cavity of capon. Layer salt over top of capon.

(continued)

3. Roast uncovered in a 400°F oven 2 hours. Remove from oven. Let stand 15 minutes.

4. Lay Dutch oven on its side. Using foil lining, gently pull salt-encased capon from Dutch oven. Break salt from capon, using an ice pick or screwdriver and hammer. Place capon on serving platter; remove vegetables from cavity. Garnish with watercress. Serve immediately.

Chicken with Poached Garlic

4 SERVINGS

1 broiler-fryer chicken (2½ to 3 pounds)
1 garlic clove, peeled and cut in half
Juice of 1 lime
Salt
Freshly ground white pepper
16 garlic cloves (unpeeled)
½ cup Chicken Stock (page 74)
¼ cup dry vermouth
Chicken Stock
2 teaspoons arrowroot
Cold water
¼ cup Mock Crème Fraîche (page 76)
1 tablespoon snipped parsley
Salt
Freshly ground white pepper

1. Rinse chicken; pat dry. Place in a roasting pan. Rub entire surface of chicken with cut garlic clove. Squeeze lime juice over chicken. Sprinkle cavity and outside of chicken lightly with salt and pepper. Place remaining garlic cloves around chicken; pour in ½ cup stock and ¼ cup dry vermouth.

2. Roast in a 325°F oven about 2½ hours, or until done; meat on drumstick will be very tender. Add stock if necessary to keep garlic covered. Remove chicken to platter. Cover loosely with aluminum foil. Let stand 20 minutes before carving.

3. Spoon fat from roasting pan. Add enough stock to pan to make 1 cup of liquid. Mix arrowroot with a little cold water; stir into stock. Simmer, stirring constantly, until thickened (about 3 minutes). Stir in Mock Crème Fraîche and parsley. Season to taste with salt and pepper. Pass sauce with chicken.

Note: To eat garlic cloves, gently press with fingers; the soft cooked interior will slip out. The flavor of the poached garlic is very delicate.

Chicken with Poached Garlic

Martinique Stuffed Chicken in Rum

4 TO 6
SERVINGS

1 roaster chicken (about 4 pounds)
1 lime, halved
Salt and pepper
2 white bread slices with crusts trimmed
1 cup milk
1 package (3 ounces) cream cheese
2 tablespoons amber rum
½ cup chopped chicken livers
2 pork sausage links, casing removed and meat chopped finely
1 scallion or green onion, chopped
1 tablespoon chopped parsley
⅛ teaspoon cayenne or red pepper
Salt and pepper (optional)

1. Rub chicken skin with the cut side of lime. Season with salt and pepper. Remove the fat deposits from the opening of the cavity. Set chicken and fat aside.
2. Soak bread in milk. Set aside.
3. Combine cream cheese, rum, chicken liver, sausage, scallion, parsley, and cayenne.
4. Squeeze bread and add to mixture; discard milk. Add salt and pepper, if desired. Mix well.
5. Stuff cavity of chicken with the mixture, then tie chicken legs and wings to hold close to body.
6. Place chicken, breast side up, on rack in a shallow roasting pan. Lay reserved fat across breast.
7. Roast in a 375°F oven about 2 hours.
8. Garnish with **watercress** and serve with Smothered Mixed Vegetables (page 78).

Stuffed Chicken, Jamaican Style

ABOUT
6 SERVINGS

1 roaster chicken or capon, about 6 pounds
Sweet Potato Stuffing

1. Rub cavities of chicken with a mixture of **salt** and **pepper.** Lightly fill body and neck cavities with Sweet Potato Stuffing. Truss. Brush skin thoroughly with **melted butter or margarine.**
2. Place chicken, breast up, on rack in a shallow roasting pan. Spread a piece of cheesecloth which has been dipped in melted butter or margarine over top and sides of chicken.
3. Roast uncovered at 325°F 3 to 3½ hours, or until thickest part of drumstick is tender. Keep cloth moist during roasting by brushing occasionally with fat from pan.

Sweet Potato Stuffing: Combine **1¼ cups mashed sweet potatoes, 7 slices bread,** toasted and cut into cubes, and **½ cup finely chopped celery** in a bowl. Put **6 pork sausage links** and **2 tablespoons water** into a cold skillet. Cover and cook slowly 8 to 10 minutes. Remove cover and pour off fat. With a fork break links into small pieces. Add **⅓ cup chopped onion** and cook over medium heat until onion is transparent and sausage is lightly browned. Remove from heat and stir in **1¼ teaspoons salt, ¼ teaspoon pepper, ½ teaspoon ground thyme, ¼ teaspoon sage, ¼ teaspoon crushed marjoram leaves,** and **2 tablespoons butter or margarine.** Add to sweet potato mixture and lightly mix together.
ABOUT 4½ CUPS STUFFING

Flavor-Full Broiled Chicken

Spread **chicken pieces** with an **Herb Butter, Lemon Butter,** or **Honey Glaze, below,** spreading some of the butter or glaze between skin and meat. Arrange chicken, skin side down, in a shallow baking pan or broiler pan without rack. Broil about 9 inches from source of heat 25 to 30 minutes, brushing occasionally with butter or glaze. Turn and broil, continuing to brush, 20 minutes longer, or until tender.

Herb Butters
Rosemary: Mix thoroughly with **½ cup butter or margarine,** softened, **1½ teaspoons crushed rosemary leaves** and **2 teaspoons snipped chives.**
Tarragon: Mix thoroughly with **½ cup butter or margarine,** softened, **1½ teaspoons crushed tarragon leaves.**
Herb-Garlic: Mix thoroughly with **½ cup butter or margarine,** softened, **1 clove garlic,** minced, **¾ teaspoon thyme,** and **¼ teaspoon curry powder.**
Lemon Butter: Blend **¼ cup melted butter or margarine,** **¼ cup cooking oil, 3 tablespoons lemon juice, ¼ teaspoon seasoned salt,** and **¼ teaspoon Tabasco.**
Honey Glaze: Blend **½ cup honey, ⅓ cup soy sauce, 6 tablespoons lemon juice, 2 teaspoons dry mustard,** and **2 cloves garlic,** minced.

Broiled Chicken

4 SERVINGS

2 broiler-fryer chickens, 2 pounds each
Melted butter or margarine
2 teaspoons salt
½ teaspoon pepper

1. Cook heart, gizzard, and liver for stock, if gravy is desired.
2. Split chickens into lengthwise halves. Cut away backbone and neck. Crack drumstick-joint and joints of wings. Skewer legs and wings to body.
3. Arrange chicken pieces, skin side down, in a broiler pan without rack. Brush generously with melted butter; sprinkle with a mixture of the salt, and pepper.
4. Place pan under broiler with top of chicken 7 to 9 inches from source of heat. Broil 40 to 45 minutes, or until browned.
5. Turn pieces about every 10 minutes and brush each time with melted butter.
6. Place on serving platter and pour pan juice over pieces.

Broiled Chicken with Tomatoes

SERVES 2

1 broiler-fryer
2 tablespoons butter or fat
2 tomatoes
Salt and Pepper
Sugar
4 slices bacon

1. Clean chicken and steam until tender. Split.
2. Remove ribs and as many small bones as possible without breaking meat.
3. Rub with butter.
4. Broil until crisp on the outside.
5. Cut tomatoes crosswise into halves and season with salt, pepper and sugar.

6. Broil tomatoes.
7. Fry bacon; shape into curls.
8. Serve chicken on toast; garnish with tomatoes and bacon.

Note: If desired, for sauce, brown 2 chopped onions in 2 tablespoons butter. Add 2 tablespoons each flour and tomato paste, 2 cups water, 2 bouillon cubes, 2 teaspoons Worcestershire sauce, 1 teaspoon each sugar and mustard, stirring constantly. Cook 10 minutes.

Broiled Marinated Chicken

4 SERVINGS

1 broiler-fryer chicken (2 to 2½ pounds), cut up
1 can or bottle (12 ounces) beer
2 tablespoons lemon juice
2 tablespoons oil
2 tablespoons honey
1 garlic clove, slivered
½ teaspoon crushed rosemary
½ teaspoon salt
⅛ teaspoon pepper

1. Place chicken in a shallow dish just large enough to hold pieces. Combine remaining ingredients; pour over chicken. Marinate in refrigerator at least 6 hours or overnight.
2. Grill or broil 6 to 8 inches from heat, basting often with marinade and turning, 30 to 40 minutes, or until tender.

Broiled Chicken in Lemon Juice and Oregano

4 SERVINGS

2 broiler-fryer chickens, cut up
½ cup olive oil
Juice of 2 lemons
¼ cup oregano, crushed
Salt and pepper to taste

1. Rinse chicken pieces and pat dry.
2. In a bowl, make a marinade by combining olive oil with lemon juice and oregano. Dip each piece of chicken into the marinade. Season with salt and pepper. Marinate for several hours, or overnight if possible.
3. In a preheated broiler, place the chicken fleshy side down. Broil about 6 inches from heat about 15 minutes, or until brown, basting frequently. Turn once. Broil until done.

Note: The marinade may be served as a gravy with cooked rice or noodles.

**Broiled Chicken in
Lemon Juice and Oregano**

Barbecued Chicken, Quail, or Guinea Fowl

ALLOW
½ BIRD
PER SERVING

Chicken, quail, or guinea
  fowl
Creole Barbecue Sauce (page
  75)

1. Split the birds in half and remove the backbone and neck.
2. Marinate birds overnight in Creole Barbecue Sauce.
3. Place bird halves on a grill 5 inches from glowing coals. Barbecue 25 minutes, turning several times and basting with the barbecue sauce.
4. Serve with **barbecued yams.**

Fried Chicken

3 OR 4
SERVINGS

1 frying chicken (about 3
  pounds), cut in serving
  pieces
½ cup flour
1½ teaspoons salt
¼ teaspoon pepper
Olive oil
2 eggs, well beaten
¼ cup milk
1 tablespoon chopped parsley
½ cup grated Parmesan
  cheese
1 to 2 tablespoons water

1. Rinse chicken and pat dry with paper towels. To coat chicken evenly, shake 2 or 3 pieces at a time in a plastic bag containing the flour, salt, and pepper.
2. Fill a large, heavy skillet ½-inch deep with olive oil; place over medium heat.
3. Combine eggs, milk, and parsley. Dip each chicken piece in the egg mixture and roll in cheese. Starting with meaty pieces, place the chicken, skin-side down, in the hot oil. Turn pieces as necessary to brown evenly on all sides.
4. When chicken is browned, reduce heat, pour in water, and cover pan tightly. Cook chicken slowly 25 to 40 minutes, or until all pieces are tender. For crisp skin, uncover chicken the last 10 minutes of cooking.

Crunchy Fried Chicken

4 SERVINGS

1 cup all-purpose flour
½ teaspoon salt
¼ teaspoon pepper
2 eggs
½ cup beer
1 broiler-fryer chicken (2 to
  2½ pounds), cut up
Cooking oil

1. Mix flour, salt, and pepper. Beat eggs with beer; add to flour mixture. Stir until smooth.
2. Dip chicken in batter, coating pieces well. Chill 1 hour.
3. Fry chicken in hot oil ½ to 1 inch deep 15 minutes on one side. Turn; fry on other side 5 to 10 minutes, or until browned and done. Drain on absorbent paper.

Kentucky Fried Chicken

SERVES
2 TO 4

1 broiler-fryer
1½ cups sifted flour
½ teaspoon salt
Dash pepper
1½ teaspoons baking powder
1 egg, beaten
½ cup milk

1. Cut chicken into serving portions; steam until tender.
2. Dry; refrigerate until time to fry. (If a large quantity is cooked, steam the day before.)
3. Just before frying, mix dry ingredients together; blend egg and milk.
4. Combine liquids with dry ingredients.
5. Dip pieces of seasoned chicken into batter; fry in deep fat (350°F.) until brown.
6. If very young chicken is used, it may be quartered and fried without precooking.

French-Fried Chicken: Omit batter. Dip cooked chicken into crumbs, then into egg mixed with 2 tablespoons milk, and again into crumbs.

Oriental Oven-Fried Chicken

6 SERVINGS

2 tablespoons soy sauce
2 tablespoons honey
1 tablespoon lemon juice
1 clove garlic, minced
3 pounds chicken pieces for frying
¾ cup flour
¾ cup all-vegetable shortening, melted in a skillet
2 cans (3 ounces each) chow mein noodles, finely crushed

1. In a large bowl or dish, mix the soy sauce, honey, lemon juice, and garlic. Put chicken into marinade and turn pieces to coat. Cover and refrigerate 2 to 3 hours, turning pieces once or twice.
2. Remove chicken and coat with flour (shake in a plastic bag, if desired). Dip pieces in melted shortening and then coat with crushed noodles. Arrange chicken pieces, skin side down, one layer deep in a large shallow baking dish; pour any remaining shortening over chicken.
3. Bake at 375°F 30 minutes. Turn chicken pieces over and bake about 15 minutes, or until tender.

Chicken Breasts Regina

4 SERVINGS

2 whole chicken breasts, skinned, boned, and cut in half
4 thin slices ham
4 thin slices liver sausage or liver pâté
Water
Flour
1 egg, beaten
Fine dry bread crumbs
3 tablespoons butter
Madeira Sauce (page 75)

1. Split chicken breast halves lengthwise, but not completely through. Open breast halves and pound until very thin.
2. Place a slice of ham, then a slice of liver sausage in center of each breast. Fold in half, enclosing the ham and liver sausage, moisten the edges with water, and press together.
3. Coat chicken breasts with flour, dip in beaten egg, and coat with bread crumbs.
4. Fry in butter in a skillet until golden brown on both sides. Serve with hot Madeira Sauce.

Spiced Fruited Chicken

6 TO 8 SERVINGS

1½ teaspoons salt
¼ teaspoon pepper
¼ teaspoon cinnamon
¼ teaspoon cloves
2 cloves garlic, minced
2 frying chickens, cut in serving pieces
¼ cup oil
½ cup chopped onion
½ cup raisins
½ cup crushed pineapple
2 cups orange juice
½ cup dry sherry

1. Combine salt, pepper, cinnamon, cloves, and garlic. Rub into chicken pieces.
2. Heat oil in a heavy skillet. Brown chicken in hot oil. Place browned chicken in a Dutch oven or heavy saucepot.
3. Cook onion in remaining oil in skillet until soft (about 5 minutes).
4. Add onion to chicken along with raisins, pineapple, and orange juice. Add water, if needed, to just cover chicken. Bring to boiling, reduce heat, cover, and cook until chicken is tender (about 1 hour). Add sherry and cook about 5 minutes longer to blend flavors.

Arroz con Pollo

4 SERVINGS

2 pounds chicken parts
2 tablespoons salad oil
1 can (13½ ounces) chicken broth
1 can (16 ounces) tomatoes, cut up
½ cup chopped onion
2 medium cloves garlic, minced
1 teaspoon salt
¼ teaspoon saffron or turmeric
⅛ teaspoon pepper
1 bay leaf
1 package (10 ounces) frozen peas
1 cup uncooked regular rice
¼ cup sliced pimento-stuffed or ripe olives

1. In a skillet, brown chicken in oil; pour off fat. Add broth, tomatoes, onion, garlic, salt, saffron, pepper, and bay leaf.
2. Cover; cook over low heat 15 minutes. Add remaining ingredients.
3. Cover; cook 30 minutes more or until chicken and rice are tender; stir occasionally. Remove bay leaf.

Country Style Chicken

ABOUT 4 SERVINGS

1 frying chicken (about 3 pounds), cut in serving pieces
2 tablespoons butter
2 tablespoons olive oil
1 medium-size onion, sliced
1 teaspoon salt
⅛ teaspoon pepper
1 pound zucchini
2 large green peppers
1½ tablespoons olive oil
1 teaspoon chopped basil leaves, or ¼ teaspoon dried sweet basil
½ cup dry white wine

1. In a large skillet, brown the chicken in butter and 2 tablespoons olive oil. Place onion around chicken; sprinkle with salt and pepper. Cover and cook slowly about 15 minutes.
2. While chicken is cooking, wash and cut zucchini in 1½-inch-thick slices. Wash peppers; remove stems and seeds. Rinse in cold water and slice lengthwise into 1-inch-wide strips.
3. In another skillet, heat 1½ tablespoons olive oil and sauté zucchini and peppers until soft (about 10 minutes). Sprinkle with basil. Transfer vegetables to skillet with chicken and pour in wine.
4. Simmer, covered, about 15 minutes, or until chicken is very tender and vegetables are cooked.

Chicken with Rice

6 TO 8 SERVINGS

1 broiler-fryer chicken, (2 to 3 pounds), cut in pieces
¼ cup fat
½ cup chopped onion
1 clove garlic, minced
1 large tomato, chopped
3 cups hot water
1 cup uncooked rice
1 tablespoon minced parsley
2 teaspoons salt
½ teaspoon paprika
¼ teaspoon pepper
¼ teaspoon saffron
1 bay leaf

1. Rinse chicken and pat dry with absorbent paper.
2. Heat fat in a skillet over medium heat. Add onion and garlic; cook until onion is tender. Remove with a slotted spoon; set aside.
3. Put chicken pieces, skin side down, in skillet. Turn to brown pieces on all sides.
4. When chicken is browned, add tomato, onion, water, rice, parsley, and dry seasonings. Cover and cook over low heat about 45 minutes, or until thickest pieces of chicken are tender when pierced with a fork.

Arroz con Pollo

Basque Chicken with Olives

Chicken Cacciatore

ABOUT
6 SERVINGS

¼ cup cooking oil
1 broiler-fryer (2½ pounds),
  cut up
2 onions, sliced
2 cloves garlic, minced
3 tomatoes, cored and
  quartered
2 green peppers, sliced
1 small bay leaf
1 teaspoon salt
¼ teaspoon pepper
½ teaspoon celery seed
1 teaspoon crushed oregano
  or basil
1 can (8 ounces) tomato
  sauce
¼ cup sauterne
8 ounces spaghetti, cooked
  according to package
  directions

1. Heat oil in a large, heavy skillet; add chicken and brown on all sides. Remove from skillet.
2. Add onion and garlic to oil remaining in skillet and cook until onion is tender, but not brown; stir occasionally.
3. Return chicken to skillet and add the tomatoes, green pepper, and bay leaf.
4. Mix salt, pepper, celery seed, and oregano and blend with tomato sauce; pour over all.
5. Cover and cook over low heat 45 minutes. Blend in wine and cook, uncovered, 20 minutes longer. Discard bay leaf.
6. Put the cooked spaghetti onto a hot serving platter and top with the chicken and sauce.

Basque Chicken with Olives

4 TO 6
SERVINGS

1 broiler-fryer chicken, 3½
  pounds ready-to-cook
  weight
Salt
¼ pound fresh mushrooms
1 medium onion
½ cup small pimento-stuffed
  olives
2 tablespoons olive oil
1 tablespoon butter
2 cans (8 ounces each)
  tomato sauce
½ cup dry white wine or
  chicken broth
10 small whole onions,
  peeled
2 sprigs parsley
½ teaspoon salt
⅛ teaspoon pepper
2 medium tomatoes, peeled
  and cut in wedges
1 medium green pepper, cut
  in strips
1 tablespoon olive oil

1. Set out a Dutch oven and a skillet.
2. Rinse and pat dry the chicken with absorbent paper.
3. Sprinkle body and neck cavities with salt and set aside.
4. Clean and slice the mushrooms; set aside.
5. Chop and set aside onion.
6. Set out olives.
7. Heat the olive oil and 1 tablespoon butter in Dutch oven.
8. Add the chicken to hot fat. Fry until golden on all sides, turning with two wooden spoons. Remove chicken from Dutch oven and set aside.
9. Add the mushrooms and onions to hot fat and stir occasionally until lightly browned. Add the tomato sauce, white wine or chicken broth, 10 small onions, and 2 sprigs parsley.
10. Return chicken to Dutch oven. Sprinkle with salt and pepper.
11. Simmer, covered, 1 hour, or until chicken is tender, basting occasionally; add olives 15 minutes before end of cooking time.
12. Transfer chicken to a large platter and tuck in neck skin; keep warm.
13. Simmer sauce uncovered 5 minutes.
14. Meanwhile, prepare 2 medium tomatoes and 1 medium green pepper.
15. Heat in the skillet 1 tablespoon olive oil. Add green pepper and cook, stirring occasionally, about 2 minutes. Gently mix in tomato wedges and heat thoroughly. Arrange green pepper strips and tomato wedges around chicken. Using a slotted spoon, lift olives, onions and mushrooms from sauce and arrange on platter.
16. Serve with hot **cooked rice** and remaining sauce.

Brunswick Stew

8 SERVINGS

1 chicken (about 4 pounds), disjointed
¼ cup cooking oil
1 cup coarsely chopped onion
¼ pound salt pork, chopped
4 tomatoes, peeled and quartered
2 cups boiling water
1 cup sherry
1 bay leaf
1 teaspoon Worcestershire sauce
1½ cups fresh lima or butter beans
½ cup sliced fresh okra
1½ cups fresh bread crumbs
2 tablespoons butter
Salt to taste

1. Sauté chicken in cooking oil until golden; remove chicken. Brown onion and salt pork in the same fat.
2. Put chicken, salt pork, onion, tomatoes, boiling water, sherry, bay leaf, and Worcestershire sauce into Dutch oven or saucepot. Cover and simmer 2 hours, or until chicken is tender.
3. After 1 hour, remove bay leaf; add beans and cook about 15 minutes. Add sliced okra; continue cooking about 15 minutes.
4. Sauté fresh bread crumbs in butter; stir into stew. Add salt to taste before serving.

Chicken Tablecloth Stainer

6 TO 8 SERVINGS

2 frying chickens (about 2½ pounds each), cut in serving pieces
½ pound link sausages
½ cup canned pineapple chunks, drained
1 apple, pared, cored, and sliced
1 large, firm banana, sliced

Sauce:
2 fresh or dried ancho chilies and 2 fresh or dried pasilla chilies, or 1 tablespoon chili powder
1 cup coarsely chopped onion
1 clove garlic
2 cups (16-ounce can) tomatoes with juice
½ cup whole blanched almonds
¼ teaspoon cinnamon
⅛ teaspoon cloves
2 cups chicken stock, or 2 cups water plus 2 chicken bouillon cubes
Salt and pepper

1. Put chicken pieces into a Dutch oven or heavy kettle.
2. Fry sausages in a skillet until browned. Put into Dutch oven with chicken. Arrange pineapple, apple, and banana over chicken.
3. For sauce, first prepare chilies. (If chilies are not available, substitute chili powder.) Combine chilies, onion, garlic, tomatoes, almonds, cinnamon, and cloves in an electric blender. Blend to a smooth purée.
4. Heat the fat remaining in the skillet in which the sausages were cooked. Add the blended sauce and cook about 5 minutes, stirring constantly. Stir in chicken stock. Season to taste with salt and pepper.
5. Pour sauce over chicken in Dutch oven. Cover and simmer over low heat 1 hour, or until chicken is tender.

Chicken Tablecloth Stainer

Chicken and Dumplings (Pictured on page 25)

ABOUT
8 SERVINGS

¼ cup butter or margarine
2 broiler-fryer chickens, cut in serving-size pieces
½ cup chopped onion
¼ cup chopped celery
2 tablespoons chopped celery leaves
1 clove garlic, minced
¼ cup enriched all-purpose flour
4 cups chicken broth
1 teaspoon sugar
2 teaspoons salt
¼ teaspoon ground black pepper
1 teaspoon basil leaves
2 bay leaves
¼ cup chopped parsley
Basil Dumplings
2 packages (10 ounces each) frozen green peas

1. Heat butter in a large skillet. Add chicken pieces and brown on all sides. Remove chicken from skillet.
2. Add onion, celery, celery leaves, and garlic to fat in skillet. Cook until vegetables are tender. Sprinkle with flour and mix well. Add chicken broth, sugar, salt, pepper, basil, bay leaves, and parsley; bring to boiling, stirring constantly. Return chicken to skillet and spoon sauce over it; cover.
3. Cook in a 350°F oven 40 minutes.
4. Shortly before cooking time is completed, prepare Basil Dumplings.
5. Remove skillet from oven and turn control to 425°F. Stir peas into skillet mixture and bring to boiling. Drop dumpling dough onto stew.
6. Return to oven and cook, uncovered, 10 minutes; cover and cook 10 minutes, or until chicken is tender and dumplings are done.

Basil Dumplings: Combine **2 cups all-purpose biscuit mix** and **1 teaspoon basil leaves** in a bowl. Add **⅔ cup milk** and stir with a fork until a dough is formed. Proceed as directed in recipe.

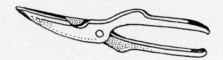

Bouillon Cocq

1 meaty smoked ham hock
1 capon (7 to 8 pounds)
½ lime
½ orange
2 tablespoons bacon drippings
1 tablespoon butter
1 tablespoon peanut oil
3 quarts water
Bouquet garni
1 pound cabbage, cut in chunks
4 small potatoes, pared and cut in chunks
2 carrots, pared and cut in chunks
2 white turnips, pared and cut in chunks
2 onions studded with 8 whole cloves
2 celery stalks, cut in pieces
2 leeks, washed and cut in chunks
Salt, pepper, and cayenne or red pepper to taste
Caribbean Rice (page 77)

1. Soak ham hock in cold water to remove excess salt. Drain.
2. Truss capon as for roasting. Rub skin with cut side of lime half, then cut side of orange half. Let stand to drain.
3. Heat bacon drippings, butter, and peanut oil in a deep soup kettle. Brown capon. Add ham hock, water, and bouquet garni; bring to a boil, reduce heat, and simmer 30 minutes, skimming twice.
4. Add vegetables and seasonings, bring to a boil, skim, then cook over low heat 30 minutes, or until vegetables and meats are tender.
5. Put the capon on a large platter and surround with drained vegetables and rice. Drink the broth from cups.

Chicken with Cheese

2 TO 4
SERVINGS

¼ cup butter
1 chicken (3 pounds), cut in
  pieces
1 medium onion, minced
Salt and pepper to taste
½ teaspoon rosemary
¼ teaspoon paprika
1 garlic clove, crushed in a
  garlic press
1½ cups chicken broth
⅓ pound kasseri cheese, cut
  in thin slices

1. Melt butter in a large skillet. Brown chicken on all sides. Add onion. Season with salt and pepper. Add rosemary, paprika, garlic, and chicken broth. Simmer, covered, about 40 minutes, or until chicken is tender.
2. Lay cheese slices on top of chicken. Simmer, covered, 5 minutes more. Serve at once.

Chicken à la King

SERVES 2

1 tablespoon butter
1 tablespoon flour
Dash white pepper
¼ teaspoon salt
½ teaspoon paprika
1 cup milk or diluted
  evaporated milk
¼ cup cream
1 cup cooked chicken, cut
  in pieces
2 olives, chopped
1 pimiento, chopped

1. Melt butter and blend in next four ingredients.
2. Heat to bubbling.
3. Stir in milk and cream.
4. Cook, stirring constantly, until sauce thickens.
5. Cook 2 minutes longer.
6. Add chicken, olives and pimiento and heat thoroughly.
7. Serve on toast, baking powder biscuits, in patty shells or bread croustades.

Note: If desired, omit olives. Add 1 tablespoon sherry, 1 8-oz. can sliced mushrooms and 1 tablespoon chopped green pepper.

Chicken Marengo

4 OR 5
SERVINGS

1 broiler-fryer chicken (2 to
  3 pounds)
⅓ cup all-purpose flour
1 teaspoon salt
¼ teaspoon pepper
¼ cup olive oil
1 clove garlic, crushed
3 tablespoons chopped onion
4 tomatoes, quartered
1 cup white wine
Herb Bouquet
1 cup (about 4 ounces) sliced
  mushrooms
2 tablespoons butter
½ cup sliced olives
½ cup chicken bouillon
2 tablespoons all-purpose
  flour

1. Disjoint chicken and cut into serving-size pieces. Rinse and pat dry with absorbent paper.
2. Coat chicken evenly with a mixture of flour, salt, and pepper.
3. Heat oil in a large skillet and brown chicken.
4. Add garlic, onion, tomatoes, wine, and Herb Bouquet to chicken; cover and simmer over low heat about ½ hour, or until thickest pieces of chicken are tender when pierced with a fork.
5. Sauté mushrooms in butter and add to chicken with olives.
6. Put bouillon and flour into screw-top jar; cover and shake well.
7. Remove chicken from skillet and discard Herb Bouquet. Gradually add bouillon-flour liquid to mixture in skillet, stirring constantly. Boil 3 to 5 minutes until mixture thickens.
8. Return chicken to sauce; cover and simmer 10 minutes. Arrange chicken on a hot platter. Cover with the sauce.

Herb Bouquet: Tie neatly together **3 or 4 sprigs of parsley, 1 sprig thyme,** and **½ bay leaf.**

Chicken and Dumplings (page 23)

Chicken Breasts with Yogurt Sauce

6 SERVINGS

½ cup butter
6 chicken breasts, boned
Salt and pepper to taste
½ teaspoon paprika
6 fresh scallions, chopped
¼ cup minced parsley
2 cups chicken stock
Juice of 1 lemon
1 pound mushrooms, sliced
2 cups plain yogurt
1 cup coarsely ground
  walnuts

1. Melt butter in a large skillet. Add chicken and season with salt, pepper, and paprika. Brown on both sides.
2. Add scallions, parsley, chicken stock, and lemon juice; bring to a boil. Reduce heat and simmer covered about 20 minutes, or until chicken is tender.
3. Remove chicken and arrange on a serving platter.
4. Add mushrooms to the stock. Simmer uncovered 3 minutes. Blend in yogurt and walnuts. (If sauce is too thick, dilute with a little stock or water.) Heat just to warm yogurt; do not boil.
5. Pour sauce over chicken.

Braised Chicken and Onions

6 TO 8 SERVINGS

1 stewing chicken (about 4 pounds)
Papaya leaves
1 lime, halved
1 orange, halved
Salt and freshly ground pepper to taste
3 tablespoons soybean, olive, or peanut oil
3 tablespoons bacon drippings
2 tablespoons water
24 small onions
2 cups chicken stock
2 tablespoons butter
2 tablespoons cornstarch
Chopped parsley
Chopped scallions or green onions

1. Truss chicken. Wrap in papaya leaves and refrigerate for 12 hours.
2. Rub the chicken with the cut sides of the lime and orange. Season with salt and pepper.
3. Heat oil and bacon drippings in a Dutch oven. Brown chicken. Add water and cover.
4. Cook in a 375°F oven about 2 hours, or until almost tender; turn occasionally and stir the juices. Add stock if more liquid is needed.
5. Add onions and continue cooking until onions are tender and well browned (about 30 minutes).
6. Place chicken and onions on a large serving platter. Carve bird.
7. Pour stock into Dutch oven and set over medium heat to deglaze. Mix butter and cornstarch and add to stock. Stir until sauce is slightly thicker.
8. Pour sauce over meat and sprinkle with chopped parsley and scallions. Serve with Caribbean Rice (see page 77).

Royal Chicken

ABOUT 6 SERVINGS

⅓ cup butter
2 medium onions, chopped
1 cup sliced mushrooms
1 chicken or capon, cut in pieces
1 cup hot water
1 teaspoon salt
¼ teaspoon pepper
1 tablespoon flour
1 teaspoon paprika (optional)
1 cup sour cream or white wine

1. Melt butter in a large skillet. Add onion, mushrooms, and chicken pieces. Stir-fry until golden.
2. Add water, salt, and pepper.
3. Cover; cook over medium heat about 35 minutes, or until chicken is tender.
4. Blend flour, paprika (if desired), and sour cream. Stir into liquid in skillet. Bring just to boiling. Simmer 3 minutes.

Sweet and Sour Chicken

4 SERVINGS

Sauce:
¾ cup chicken stock
¼ cup brown sugar
¼ cup sugar
½ cup vinegar
¼ cup ketchup
1 tablespoon sherry
1 tablespoon cornstarch
2 tablespoons soy sauce
¼ cup pineapple juice

Chicken:
1 chicken breast, boned, skinned, and partially frozen
1 clove garlic
2 slices fresh ginger, each slice cut in quarters (1 teaspoon minced)
3 tablespoons peanut oil
1 green pepper, cut in 1-inch pieces
1 tomato, cut in 1-inch pieces
½ cup pineapple chunks, drained (reserving liquid)

1. For sauce, combine stock, sugars, vinegar, ketchup, and sherry in a saucepan. Bring to a boil, stirring to dissolve sugar.
2. Blend cornstarch, soy sauce, and pineapple juice. Stir into mixture in saucepan and cook over low heat until thickened.
3. For chicken, using **slicing disc** of food processor, slice meat. Set aside.
4. Using **steel blade,** mince garlic and ginger root by starting machine and adding ingredients through feed tube. Set aside.
5. Heat 2 tablespoons peanut oil in a wok. Add minced garlic and ginger root and stir-fry a few seconds. Add sliced chicken and stir-fry until just tender. Remove from pan and set aside.
6. Heat 1 tablespoon peanut oil in wok and stir-fry green peppers 2 to 3 minutes. Add tomato, pineapple, and chicken and stir-fry only to heat through.
7. Remove to a serving dish and spoon sauce over the top. Serve at once with **rice.**

Skillet Chicken and Vegetables

6 SERVINGS

1 can (about 10 ounces) condensed chicken broth
1 cup dry white wine, such
as chablis
1 tablespoon instant minced
onion
½ teaspoon salt
1 bay leaf
¼ teaspoon rosemary,
crushed
6 half breasts of chicken
6 small carrots
6 small zucchini
2 tablespoons cornstarch
2 tablespoons cold water
3 tablespoons chopped
pimento
2 tablespoons chopped
parsley

1. Combine broth, wine, onion, salt, bay leaf, and rosemary in a large skillet. Heat to boiling.
2. Place chicken breasts in the boiling liquid; cover and simmer 20 minutes.
3. While chicken is cooking, pare carrots and cut in half lengthwise. Cut zucchini in half lengthwise. Add carrots and zucchini to the chicken; cover, and cook 15 minutes longer, or until chicken is tender and vegetables are crisp-tender.
4. Remove chicken and vegetables with a slotted spoon; keep warm.
5. Mix cornstarch with water and stir into liquid remaining in skillet. Cook, stirring until sauce boils thoroughly. Add pimento and parsley, and pour over chicken and vegetables. Serve immediately.

Chicken Mexicana

ABOUT
6 SERVINGS

3 tablespoons vegetable oil
2 broiler-fryer chickens (2½
to 3 pounds each), cut in
serving-size pieces
2 cans (8 ounces each)
tomato sauce
1 can (13¾ ounces) chicken
broth
2 tablespoons (½ envelope)
dry onion soup mix
¾ cup chopped onion
1 clove garlic, minced
6 tablespoons crunchy
peanut butter
½ cup cream
½ teaspoon chili powder
¼ cup dry sherry
Cooked rice

1. Heat oil in a large skillet. Add chicken and brown on all sides.
2. Meanwhile, combine tomato sauce, 1 cup chicken broth, soup mix, onion, and garlic in a saucepan. Heat thoroughly, stirring constantly.
3. Pour sauce over chicken in skillet. Simmer, covered, 20 minutes.
4. Put peanut butter into a bowl and blend in cream and remaining chicken broth; stir into skillet along with chili powder and sherry. Heat thoroughly. Serve with hot fluffy rice.

Green Chicken

6 SERVINGS

1 medium onion, coarsely
chopped
1 clove garlic, peeled
1 cup (small can) salsa verde
mexicana (Mexican green
tomato sauce)
¼ cup (lightly filled) fresh
parsley
1 teaspoon salt
¼ teaspoon pepper
2 frying chickens, cut in
serving pieces

1. Put onion, garlic, salsa verde, and parsley into an electric blender. Blend until liquefied. Stir in salt and pepper.
2. Rinse chicken pieces and pat dry; arrange pieces in a heavy skillet. Pour green sauce over chicken. Cover; bring to boiling. Cook over low heat until chicken is tender, about 1 hour.

Skillet Chicken and Vegetables

Breast of Chicken Savannah

8 SERVINGS

4 large chicken breasts,
split
2½ ounces (about ¼ cup)
peanut butter
8 thin slices cooked
ham
¼ cup sherry
Parmesan Sauce:
¼ cup flour
2 cups milk
½ teaspoon salt
6 tablespoons freshly grated
Parmesan cheese
2 tablespoons firm butter

1. Lift skin on chicken breasts slightly, and spread a film of peanut butter on meat under skin; replace skin.
2. Place 1 slice of cooked ham over skin side of each breast.
3. Put sherry into a large casserole or braising pan. Add chicken pieces, ham side up; cover and cook in a 350°F oven 1 hour, or until pieces are tender.
4. Remove breasts from pan and keep warm while preparing Parmesan sauce; reserve ¼ cup pan drippings.
5. For sauce, put the pan drippings into a medium saucepan. Add flour; stir and heat until bubbly. Add milk gradually, stirring well; bring to boiling and cook 1 to 2 minutes.
6. Add salt and Parmesan cheese, stirring until cheese melts. Stir in butter, 1 tablespoon at a time.
7. Pour sauce over chicken and serve.

Chicken Curry with Rice

8 SERVINGS

⅔ cup butter or margarine
6 tablespoons chopped onion
6 tablespoons chopped celery
6 tablespoons chopped green
apple
24 peppercorns
2 bay leaves
⅔ cup all-purpose flour
5 teaspoons curry powder
½ teaspoon sugar
¼ teaspoon nutmeg
5 cups milk
4 teaspoons lemon juice
1 teaspoon Worcestershire
sauce
½ cup cream
¼ cup sherry
½ teaspoon Worcestershire
sauce
6 cups cubed cooked chicken
Hot cooked rice

1. Heat butter in a heavy 3-quart saucepan over low heat. Add onion, celery, apple, peppercorns, and bay leaves, and cook over medium heat until lightly browned, occasionally moving and turning with a spoon.
2. Blend in flour, curry powder, sugar, and nutmeg; heat until mixture bubbles.
3. Remove from heat and add milk gradually, stirring constantly.
4. Return to heat and bring rapidly to boiling. Stirring constantly, cook until mixture thickens; cook 1 to 2 minutes longer.
5. Remove from heat; add lemon juice and 1 teaspoon Worcestershire sauce. Strain mixture through a fine sieve, pressing vegetables against sieve to extract all sauce. Set sauce aside.
6. Reheat the curry sauce and blend in cream, sherry, and ½ teaspoon Worcestershire sauce; add chicken and cook over medium heat 2 to 3 minutes, or until mixture is thoroughly heated. Serve with rice.

Capon in Cream

ABOUT
6 SERVINGS

1 capon or chicken (5 to 6
pounds)
Salt
2 cups chicken stock or
broth
4 egg yolks
1 tablespoon melted butter
4 teaspoons flour
2 cups sour cream
1 teaspoon salt
¼ teaspoon pepper

1. Sprinkle cavity of bird with salt. Place in a large kettle.
2. Add stock to kettle. Cover. Simmer until just tender (about 1 hour). Allow to cool.
3. Meanwhile, cream egg yolks and butter; add flour and blend thoroughly. Stir in sour cream. Season with 1 teaspoon salt and pepper. Beat at high speed until stiff. Cook until thickened in top of a double boiler, stirring constantly to keep from curdling or sticking (handle like hollandaise sauce). Cool.
4. Make cuts in capon as for carving, but without cutting through. Place in a shallow baking pan. Fill cuts with sauce, then spread remainder over the whole surface of the bird.

5. Bake at 425°F about 20 minutes, or until sauce is browned.
6. Meanwhile, boil liquid in which chicken was cooked until it is reduced to 1 cup of stock.
7. To serve, pour stock over capon. Carve at the table.

Chicken and Tomato Casserole

4 SERVINGS

1 broiler-fryer chicken (about 3 pounds), cut up
3 tablespoons shortening
½ cup chopped onion
¼ cup chopped green pepper
1 can (28 ounces) tomatoes (undrained)
1 can (8 ounces) tomato sauce
1 can (6 ounces) tomato paste
1 teaspoon salt
1 teaspoon oregano

1. Brown chicken in shortening in a skillet. Place in a 2-quart casserole.
2. Sauté onion and green pepper in fat in skillet. Stir in remaining ingredients and pour over chicken.
3. Bake, covered, at 350°F 1 hour, or until chicken is tender. Serve with **hot, cooked spaghetti.**

Chicken Artichoke Casserole

6 SERVINGS

⅓ cup butter or margarine
¼ cup flour
1¾ cups milk
Dash ground red pepper
1 garlic clove, minced
¼ cup (1 ounce) shredded Cheddar cheese
1½ ounces Gruyère cheese, cut up
2 cups chopped cooked chicken
1 can (4 ounces) button mushrooms, drained
1 can (14 ounces) artichoke hearts, drained

1. Melt butter in a saucepan. Stir in flour. Gradually add milk, stirring until thickened and smooth.
2. Add red pepper, garlic, and cheese, stirring until smooth. Blend in chicken, mushrooms, and artichoke hearts. Pour into a 2-quart casserole.
3. Bake, covered, at 350°F 30 minutes, or until heated through. Sprinkle with **paprika.**

Piquant Chicken

4 SERVINGS

1 frying chicken, cut in serving pieces
Butter or margarine
6 limes or 4 lemons, sliced as thinly as possible
Salt and pepper

1. Brown chicken pieces in butter in a skillet.
2. Place chicken in an ovenproof casserole. Cover completely with lime or lemon slices. Sprinkle with salt and pepper. Cover tightly with foil.
3. Bake at 325°F about 1¼ hours, or until chicken is tender.

Mexican Chili Chicken Casserole

8 SERVINGS

¼ cup instant minced onion
½ teaspoon instant minced garlic
⅓ cup water
1 can (17 ounces) whole kernel corn
2 tablespoons oil
1 can (16 ounces) tomatoes, drained and broken up
1 can (8 ounces) tomato sauce
4 teaspoons chili powder
1 teaspoon oregano leaves, crumbled
⅛ teaspoon salt
1 tablespoon cornstarch
½ cup pitted ripe olives, sliced
1½ pounds boned cooked chicken, chunked
8 bacon slices, cooked crisp

1. Combine minced onion and garlic with water; let stand for 10 minutes to rehydrate. Drain and reserve liquid from corn; set corn and liquid aside separately.
2. In a large saucepan, heat oil. Add onion and garlic; sauté for 5 minutes. Stir in tomatoes, tomato sauce, chili powder, oregano leaves, and salt.
3. Mix cornstarch with reserved corn liquid; stir into saucepan. Simmer, uncovered, for 15 minutes, stirring occasionally. Remove from heat; add olives.
4. In a large casserole, place in layers chicken, reserved corn, and sauce. Repeat procedure, ending with corn. Garnish with crisp bacon slices over top.
5. Bake at 400°F until casserole is bubbly (about 20 minutes).

Chicken-Green Noodle Casserole

8 SERVINGS

½ cup chopped onion
½ cup slivered almonds
1 cup sliced fresh mushrooms
¼ cup butter or margarine
3 cups cooked spinach (green) noodles
1 cup milk
2 cans (10¾ ounces each) condensed cream of chicken soup
3 cups chopped cooked chicken
¼ teaspoon pepper
⅓ cup buttered bread crumbs

1. Sauté onion, almonds, and mushrooms in butter in a skillet. Combine with remaining ingredients, except bread crumbs. Put into a 2½-quart casserole.
2. Bake, covered, at 350°F 30 minutes. Remove cover. Sprinkle with bread crumbs and bake an additional 15 minutes, or until heated through.

Chicken Surprise

4 SERVINGS

½ cup chopped onion
1 tablespoon butter or margarine
1 tablespoon cornstarch
¾ cup orange juice
2 tablespoons prepared mustard
½ cup sherry
2 cups chopped cooked chicken
½ cup raisins
½ cup sliced celery

1. Sauté onion in butter in a skillet. Stir in cornstarch. Gradually add orange juice, mustard and sherry, stirring until thickened and smooth.
2. Place chicken, raisins, and celery in a 1-quart casserole. Pour sauce over all; mix.
3. Bake, covered, at 325°F 30 minutes, or until heated through. Serve in **chow mein noodle** or **patty shells** and garnish with **orange twists**.

Mexican Chili Chicken Casserole

Country-Flavored Chicken Halves

4 SERVINGS

1 package 15-minute chicken
   marinade
1 cup cold water
1 broiler-fryer (2½ to 3
   pounds), cut in half

1. In a shallow pan, thoroughly blend chicken marinade and water. Place well-drained chicken in marinade; turn, pierce all surfaces of chicken deeply with fork. Marinade only 15 minutes, turning several times. Remove chicken from marinade and arrange skin side up in a shallow ungreased pan just large enough to accommodate the chicken.
2. Bake uncovered, at 425°F for 45 to 55 minutes, until thoroughly cooked.

Chicken Polish Style

ABOUT
4 SERVINGS

1 chicken (2 to 3 pounds)
Salt
Chicken livers
¾ cup dry bread crumbs
1 egg
1 teaspoon dill weed
¼ teaspoon pepper
½ cup milk (about)
⅓ cup melted butter

1. Sprinkle the chicken with salt. Let stand 1 hour.
2. Chop the livers finely. Combine with bread crumbs, egg, salt to taste, dill, pepper, and as much milk as needed for a loose, sour-cream-like consistency.
3. Fill cavity of chicken with crumb mixture; truss. Place chicken in roasting pan.
4. Bake at 400°F about 45 minutes, or until chicken is tender. Baste often with melted butter.

Chicken with Ham: Prepare Chicken Polish Style as directed. Substitute **6 ounces (1 cup) ground ham, ½ cup sliced mushrooms,** and **2 crushed juniper berries** for the chicken livers. Add **½ cup sherry** to pan drippings for a sauce.

Chicken and Wild Rice

8 SERVINGS

¾ cup uncooked wild rice
4 cups chopped cooked
   chicken
1 cup sherry
1 cup chicken broth
1 small onion, chopped
1 can (8 ounces) mushroom
   slices, drained
¼ cup butter or margarine,
   melted
1 can (10¾ ounces) con-
   densed cream of mushroom
   soup
1 can (10¾ ounces) condensed cream of chicken soup
2 packages (10 ounces each)
   frozen broccoli or
   asparagus spears, cooked
   and drained
1 cup (4 ounces) shredded
   Cheddar cheese

1. Cook wild rice according to package directions.
2. Combine rice with remaining ingredients, except broccoli and cheese.
3. Spread half the rice mixture in a 13x9-inch baking dish. Top with broccoli. Evenly spread remaining rice mixture over all.
4. Bake, uncovered, at 350°F 45 minutes, or until heated through. Sprinkle with cheese and bake an additional 5 minutes, or until cheese is melted.

Country-Flavored Chicken Halves

Chicken Easy Oriental Style

4 SERVINGS

¼ cup flour
1 teaspoon salt
¼ teaspoon pepper
4 chicken breasts, split in halves
¼ cup shortening
1 can (10¾ ounces) condensed cream of chicken soup
¼ cup dry white wine
¼ cup milk
1 can (4 ounces) water chestnuts, drained and sliced
¼ teaspooon ground ginger

1. Combine flour, salt, and pepper; coat chicken with mixture.
2. Brown chicken in shortening in skillet. Place in a 13x9-inch baking dish.
3. Combine soup, wine, milk, chestnuts, and ginger. Pour over chicken.
4. Bake, covered, at 350°F 1 hour, or until chicken is tender. If desired, sprinkle with snipped parsley.

Chicken en Cocotte

4 SERVINGS

1½ cups sliced leeks, white part only
1 medium zucchini, cut in ¼-inch slices
2 large sweet red or green peppers, cut in ¼-inch slices
1 large green pepper, cut in ¼-inch strips
2 teaspoons snipped fresh or 1 teaspoon finely crushed dried rosemary leaves
2 teaspoons snipped fresh or 1 teaspoon finely crushed dried thyme leaves
1½ teaspoons salt
⅓ cup dry sauterne or other white wine
1 roasting chicken (about 3 pounds)
1 teaspoon clarified butter
Salt
1 small bunch parsley
1 cup 3-inch pieces, leek, green part only
1 tablespoon dry sauterne or other white wine

1. Arrange 1½ cups leeks, the zucchini, and peppers in bottom of a Dutch oven. Mix rosemary, thyme, and 1½ teaspoons salt; sprinkle one third of herb mixture over vegetables. Pour ⅓ cup sauterne over vegetables.
2. Rinse chicken and pat dry. Rub chicken with butter and sprinkle with remaining herb mixture. Lightly salt cavity of chicken. Stuff cavity with parsley and green part of leeks; sprinkle with 1 tablespoon sauterne. Place chicken in Dutch oven; cover with lid.
3. Bake at 325°F 2 hours, or until tender. Remove chicken to platter; discard parsley and leek from cavity. Surround chicken with vegetables.

Crispy Chicken with Curried Fruit

4 SERVINGS

1 cup corn flake crumbs
½ teaspoon salt
Dash pepper
1 broiler-fryer chicken (about 3 pounds), cut up
½ cup evaporated milk
Curried Fruit

1. Combine crumbs, salt, and pepper. Dip chicken pieces in milk. Roll in crumb mixture. Place chicken pieces in a 1½-quart shallow baking dish.
2. Bake, uncovered, at 350°F with Curried Fruit 1 hour, or until chicken is tender.

Curried Fruit

4 SERVINGS

1 can (16 ounces) peach halves, drained*
1 can (8½ ounces) pineapple chunks, drained*
4 maraschino cherries
¼ cup butter or margarine, melted
½ cup firmly packed brown sugar
1 tablespoon curry powder

1. Put fruits into a 1½-quart casserole. Combine butter, brown sugar, and curry powder. Spoon over fruits.
2. Bake, covered, at 350°F 1 hour. Serve with **hot, cooked rice.**

*The drained liquids can be refrigerated and used in gelatin salads.

Crispy Chicken with Curried Fruit

Herb-Chicken with Mushrooms

ABOUT
4 SERVINGS

2 tablespoons butter or margarine
1 broiler-fryer chicken (3 pounds), cut in quarters
¾ cup cider vinegar
¼ cup water
1 cup (about 3 ounces) sliced mushrooms
1 tablespoon finely chopped parsley
1 tablespoon finely chopped chives
1 teaspoon crushed tarragon
½ teaspoon thyme
½ teaspoon salt
¼ teaspoon black pepper
2 tablespoons flour
1½ cups chicken broth
½ cup sherry

1. Heat butter in a large skillet. Place chicken pieces, skin side down, in skillet and brown on all sides.
2. Meanwhile, pour a mixture of vinegar and water over the mushrooms. Let stand 10 minutes; drain.
3. When chicken is evenly browned, transfer pieces to a shallow baking dish. Sprinkle the seasonings over the chicken. Spoon drained mushrooms over the top; sprinkle evenly with flour. Pour broth and wine over all.
4. Bake at 325°F about 1 hour, or until tender.

Chicken Novaes

12 SERVINGS

2 jars (6 ounces each) tamales
1 can (4 ounces) sliced mushrooms, drained
2 cans (8 ounces each) tomato sauce
12 slices cooked chicken
2 cups cooked white rice
1 cup chopped green onion
2 cans (10¾ ounces each) condensed cream of chicken soup
1 cup (4 ounces) shredded Cheddar cheese
½ cup buttered bread crumbs

1. Remove paper from tamales. Cut in half crosswise and arrange in bottom of a 3-quart casserole.
2. Over the tamales, layer mushrooms, 1 can tomato sauce, chicken, rice and onion. Top with the remaining can of tomato sauce. Spoon chicken soup over all, inserting a knife so soup will seep through.
3. Combine cheese and bread crumbs. Sprinkle over top of casserole mixture.
4. Bake, covered, at 350°F 30 minutes, or until bubbly.

Chicken Breasts with Sour Cream

8 SERVINGS

8 chicken breasts, split in halves, boned, and skin removed
16 bacon slices
3 packages (3 ounces each) smoked sliced beef
1 can (10¾ ounces) condensed cream of mushroom soup
2 cups sour cream

1. Roll each chicken breast in 1 bacon slice. (Another half bacon slice may be needed if the breast is a large one, so that all of it will be surrounded by the bacon.)
2. Shred beef and place in a 13x9-inch baking dish. Top with chicken breasts.
3. Combine soup and sour cream. Spoon over chicken breasts.
4. Bake, uncovered, at 275°F 3 hours, or until chicken is tender. Cover lightly with foil if it begins to get too brown.

Chicken Mac

4 SERVINGS

1 package (7¼ ounces) macaroni and cheese dinner
1 tablespoon instant minced onion
2 tablespoons chopped celery
2 tablespoons chopped green pepper
1 garlic clove, minced
2 tablespoons butter or margarine
1 can (8¾ ounces) whole kernel corn, drained
1 can (10¾ ounces) condensed cream of chicken soup
1½ cups chopped cooked chicken or turkey
2 tablespoons snipped parsley
⅓ cup buttered bread crumbs

1. Prepare dinner according to package directions, except use ½ cup milk.
2. Sauté onion, celery, green pepper, and garlic in butter in a skillet. Combine with corn, soup, chicken, and prepared dinner. Put into a greased 1½-quart casserole.
3. Combine parsley and bread crumbs. Sprinkle over top of casserole mixture.
4. Bake, covered, at 350°F 25 minutes, or until heated through.

Chicken Vesuvio

4 SERVINGS

1 broiler-fryer chicken (2 to 3 pounds), cut in pieces
½ cup flour
1½ teaspoons salt
¼ teaspoon pepper
½ cup olive oil
2 tablespoons olive oil
1 clove garlic, sliced
2 tablespoons Marsala
½ teaspoon chopped parsley
Deep-Fried Potatoes

1. Coat chicken pieces with a mixture of flour, salt, and pepper.
2. Heat ½ cup oil in a large skillet. Add chicken pieces and brown on all sides. Put into a large, shallow baking dish.
3. Heat 2 tablespoons oil and garlic until garlic is lightly browned. Add Marsala and parsley; mix well. Pour over chicken in baking dish.
4. Bake at 325°F about 45 minutes, or until chicken is tender; turn once.
5. Prepare potatoes and place around edges of baking dish.

Chicken and Rice Valencia

4 SERVINGS

1 broiler-fryer chicken (about 3 pounds), cut up
¼ cup olive oil
1 medium onion, finely chopped
1 medium green pepper, slivered
1 can (10 ounces) tomatoes (undrained)
1 bay leaf
¾ cup water
Dash ground saffron (optional)
1 cup drained stuffed olives
1 package (6 ounces) Spanish rice mix
½ cup chopped celery

1. Brown chicken pieces in olive oil in a skillet.
2. Add remaining ingredients, except rice and celery. Place in a 2-quart casserole.
3. Bake, covered, at 350°F 1 hour, or until chicken is tender.
4. Meanwhile, prepare rice according to package directions. Stir celery into rice. Spread on hot serving platter.
5. Remove bay leaf from chicken. Spoon chicken and sauce over rice.

Chicken Tetrazzini

Chicken Tetrazzini

SERVES 6

1 (3 pound) broiler chicken
2 cups water
1 cup dry white wine
2 carrots, cubed
1 medium finely chopped
  onion
2 parsley stalks
½ teaspoon thyme
1½ teaspoons salt
4 tablespoons butter
5 tablespoons flour
3 cups chicken stock
4 ounces light cream
6 ounces grated Parmesan
  cheese
1 cup sliced mushrooms
8 ounces ribbon macaroni

1. Place chicken in a casserole. Add water, wine, carrots, onion, parsley, thyme and salt. Bring to a boil, skim and let boil gently for about 40 minutes with casserole covered.
2. Strain the stock and save.
3. Skin and bone the chicken when cold. Cut the meat in slices.
4. Melt 3 tablespoons butter in a saucepan. Add the flour and stir. Add in turns 3 cups stock. Add the cream and heat for about 5 minutes. Stir in the Parmesan cheese, but save some for the top.
5. Preheat the oven to 350°F.
6. Melt the rest of the butter in a frying pan and brown the mushrooms lightly.
7. Bring 2 quarts of water with 3 teaspoons salt to a boil. Add the ribbon macaroni and boil until just soft, but no more.
8. Wash the macaroni and drain.
9. Mix mushrooms and macaroni and place at the bottom of a large ovenproof dish. Put the chicken on top. Pour on the sauce. Sprinkle with the remaining cheese.
10. Bake in the oven for about 15 minutes.

Chicken-Chip Bake

4 TO 6
SERVINGS

2 cups chopped cooked
  chicken
2 cups sliced celery
1 can (8 ounces) pineapple
  chunks, drained
¾ cup mayonnaise
⅓ cup toasted slivered
  almonds
2 tablespoons lemon juice
2 teaspoons finely chopped
  onion
½ teaspoon salt
½ cup (2 ounces) shredded
  American cheese
1 cup crushed potato chips

1. Combine chicken, celery, pineapple, mayonnaise, almonds, lemon juice, onion, and salt. Put into a 1½-quart casserole. Sprinkle with cheese and potato chips.
2. Bake, uncovered, at 350°F 30 minutes, or until heated through.

Swiss Chicken Bake

6 SERVINGS

6 chicken breasts, split in
  halves, boned, and skin
  removed
1½ cups (6 ounces) shredded
  Swiss cheese
1 can (10¾ ounces) condensed cream of chicken
  soup
½ cup sherry
3 cups packaged herb stuffing mix
1 tablespoon butter or
  margarine

1. Place chicken breasts in a 13x9-inch baking dish. Sprinkle with cheese.
2. Combine soup and sherry; pour over Swiss cheese. Evenly spoon dressing over all. Dot with butter.
3. Bake, covered, at 350°F 1 hour, or until chicken is tender.

Chicken Italiano

6 FILLED
CRÊPES

2 whole chicken breasts
(about 1 pound)
2 tablespoons oil
½ pound mushrooms,
cleaned and chopped
1 can (16 ounces) stewed
tomatoes
1 medium clove garlic,
crushed in a garlic press
1 teaspoon oregano
½ teaspoon thyme
1 can (8 ounces) tomato
sauce
⅓ cup grated Parmesan
cheese
Salt and pepper
6 dinner crêpes (page 77)

1. Bone chicken and cut into 1-inch strips.
2. Heat oil, sauté chicken and mushrooms until chicken turns white. Stir in stewed tomatoes, garlic, oregano, thyme, tomato sauce, and 3 tablespoons grated cheese. Add salt and pepper to taste. Simmer, uncovered, 5 minutes.
3. Using a slotted spoon, spoon onto crêpes. Assemble, using tube method (page #), place on a baking sheet, and sprinkle tops of crêpes with remaining cheese.
4. Bake at 375°F until cheese browns (about 15 minutes). Serve immediately with any remaining sauce.

Chicken-Cheese Pies

MAKES
4 INDIVIDUAL PIES

Pastry for 2-crust pie (your
favorite recipe or a prepared
mix)
   1 chicken bouillon cube
     dissolved in ½ cup
     boiling water
   2 cups diced cooked
     chicken
   1 4-oz. can sliced
     mushrooms, drained
   ¼ cup butter or margarine
   ¼ cup chopped onion
   3 tablespoons flour
   ¼ teaspoon salt
   ¼ teaspoon garlic salt
   ¼ teaspoon pepper
   1 cup cream
   ½ teaspoon Worcestershire
     sauce
   ¼ cup grated Cheddar
     cheese

1. Line 4 small individual pie pans with pastry; set aside.
2. Heat ¼ cup butter in skillet.
3. Add onion and cook until soft.
4. Blend in flour and the next 3 ingredients; heat until mixture is bubbly; stir in the chicken broth, cream and Worcestershire sauce.
5. Cook, stirring constantly until well blended; stir in chicken and mushrooms; set aside to cool.
6. Spoon ¼ of filling into each pastry shell; sprinkle grated cheese over each.
7. Roll out pastry for top crusts and cut into circles ¾ inch larger than pie pans.
8. Tuck extra dough under lower crust and flute edge or press with tines of fork.
9. Bake pies at 450°F. 15 to 20 minutes, or until delicately browned.

Chicken Pie

6 SERVINGS

1¼ cups water
1 cup milk
1 package (⅞ ounce) chicken
gravy mix
1 package (10 ounces) frozen
peas, thawed
2 tablespoons chopped
pimento
2 cups cubed cooked chicken
1 tablespoon finely chopped
onion
1 teaspoon snipped parsley
2 cups all-purpose biscuit
mix

1. Combine ¾ cup water, milk, and gravy mix in a saucepan; bring to a boil.
2. Stir in peas, pimento, and chicken; heat thoroughly.
3. Stir onion, parsley, and remaining ½ cup water into biscuit mix, stirring until thoroughly moistened.
4. Pour hot chicken mixture into an 11x7-inch shallow baking dish. Roll or pat out dough to fit top of baking dish. Set on chicken mixture.
5. Bake, uncovered, at 450°F 10 to 12 minutes, or until topping is golden brown.

Chicken Italiano

Old-Fashioned Chicken Pie

6 TO 8
SERVINGS

1 stewing chicken, 4 to 5 pounds, cut up
1 small onion
2 pieces (3 inches each) celery with leaves
3 sprigs parsley
2 teaspoons salt
2 or 3 peppercorns
1 small bay leaf
4 medium-sized potatoes, pared and quartered
4 carrots, scraped and sliced
3 stalks celery, cut in pieces
2 small onions
¼ to ½ teaspoon salt
Biscuit dough (made from 1½ cups flour, or use a mix), rolled out

1. Put chicken pieces into a 4-quart kettle. Add **1 quart hot water,** 1 onion, 2 pieces celery, parsley, 2 teaspoons salt, peppercorns, and bay leaf. Cover; bring to boiling; remove foam. Cover tightly and simmer 2 to 3 hours, or until thickest pieces are fork-tender.
2. Remove chicken from broth and cool slightly; remove meat from bones. Cut meat in 1-inch pieces. Set aside. Strain and cool broth; remove fat. Reserve broth.
3. Bring reserved chicken broth to boiling. Add the vegetables and salt. Cook, covered, about 20 minutes, or until tender. Remove vegetables with slotted spoon and place in a 2-quart deep casserole along with the chicken pieces.
4. To prepare gravy, combine ½ **cup water** and ¼ **cup flour** in a jar. Cover and shake until blended. Stirring constantly, add gradually to boiling broth; cook and stir 3 to 5 minutes.
5. Pour gravy into casserole. (There should be enough gravy to "float" chicken and vegetable pieces without mixture being too liquid.) Top with cutout biscuits placed so they just touch.
6. Bake at 425°F 15 to 20 minutes, or until biscuits are golden brown.

Chicken or Turkey Mole Poblano

ABOUT
4 CUPS
FILLING
(ENOUGH FOR
3½ DOZEN
TAMALES)

6 ancho chilies, fresh or dried
2 cups (16-ounce can) cooked tomatoes
1 large onion, coarsely chopped
1 clove garlic, peeled
½ cup salted peanuts or ½ cup peanut butter
1 tortilla or 1 piece of toast, torn in pieces
⅓ cup raisins
2 tablespoons sesame seed
¼ cup oil
1 tablespoon sugar
¼ teaspoon anise
¼ teaspoon cinnamon
¼ teaspoon cloves
¼ teaspoon coriander
¼ teaspoon cumin (comino)
1 cup chicken or turkey stock
1 ounce (1 square) unsweetened chocolate
Salt and pepper
3 cups diced cooked chicken or turkey

1. Prepare chilies. Combine with tomatoes, onion, garlic, peanuts, tortilla, raisins, and sesame seed. Put a small amount at a time into an electric blender and blend to make a thick purée.
2. Heat oil in a large skillet. Add the purée and cook, stirring constantly, about 5 minutes. Stir in sugar, anise, cinnamon, cloves, coriander, cumin, and stock. Bring to boiling, reduce heat, and simmer. Add chocolate and continue simmering, stirring constantly, until chocolate is melted and blended into sauce. Add salt and pepper to taste. Stir in chicken pieces and simmer about 10 minutes.
3. To use as a tamale filling, the sauce must be fairly thick, so it may be simmered until desired consistency is reached. Then spoon poultry pieces and a little sauce onto tamale dough spread on a corn husk. Use leftover sauce to serve over cooked tamales.
4. Or, Chicken or Turkey Mole Poblano may be served over **hot rice.**

Chicken in Filo

8 TO 10
SERVINGS

1 stewing chicken, cut in pieces
½ cup unsalted butter
1 medium onion, minced
½ cup finely chopped leek
1 celery stalk, minced
1 garlic clove, crushed in a garlic press
2 tablespoons finely chopped parsley
2 tablespoons pine nuts
3 tablespoons flour
2½ cups chicken stock
½ cup cream
4 eggs, beaten until frothy
¼ teaspoon nutmeg
½ teaspoon dill
2 tablespoons white wine
Salt and pepper
1 package filo
Additional butter for filo

1. Rinse chicken pieces. In a large heavy Dutch oven, add ¼ cup butter. When hot, add the chicken. Cover. Cook, turning, without browning, for about 15 minutes.
2. Remove the chicken pieces and cool slightly. Remove bones and skin from chicken and discard. Chop chicken meat. Set aside.
3. Melt 2 tablespoons butter in a skillet. Add onion, leek, celery, garlic, parsley, and pine nuts. Sauté until vegetables are limp.
4. Melt remaining butter in a saucepan and blend in flour. Cook 2 minutes. Stir in stock. Simmer until sauce boils. Cool. Stir in cream, eggs, nutmeg, dill, chicken, vegetables, and wine, if sauce seems too thick. Season with salt and pepper.
5. Butter a 12x9x3-inch baking pan. Line it with 6 sheets of filo, brushing each with butter.
6. Spread chicken filling evenly over filo. Top with filo according to directions.
7. Bake at 350°F about 50 minutes, or until golden in color. Let stand 15 minutes before cutting into squares. Serve warm.

Chicken Mousse Amandine

8 SERVINGS

½ cup dry white wine, such as sauterne
2 envelopes unflavored gelatin
3 egg yolks
1 cup milk
1 cup chicken broth
½ cup (about 3 ounces) almonds, finely chopped
3 cups ground cooked chicken
¼ cup mayonnaise
2 tablespoons minced parsley
2 tablespoons chopped green olives
1 teaspoon lemon juice
1 teaspoon onion juice
½ teaspoon salt
½ teaspoon celery salt
Few grains paprika
Few grains cayenne pepper
½ cup chilled heavy cream
Sprigs of parsley

1. Place a small bowl and a rotary beater in refrigerator to chill.
2. Pour wine into a small cup and sprinkle gelatin evenly over wine; set aside.
3. Beat egg yolks slightly in top of a double boiler; add milk gradually, stirring constantly.
4. Stir in the chicken broth gradually. Cook over simmering water, stirring constantly and rapidly until mixture coats a metal spoon.
5. Remove from heat. Stir softened gelatin and immediately stir it into the hot mixture until gelatin is completely dissolved. Cool; chill in refrigerator or over ice and water until gelatin mixture begins to gel (becomes slightly thicker). If mixture is placed over ice and water, stir frequently; if placed in refrigerator, stir occasionally.
6. Blend almonds and chicken into chilled custard mixture along with mayonnaise, parsley, olives, lemon juice, onion juice, and a mixture of salt, celery salt, paprika, and cayenne pepper.
7. Using the chilled bowl and beater, beat cream until of medium consistency (piles softly).
8. Fold whipped cream into chicken mixture. Turn into a 1½-quart fancy mold. Chill in refrigerator until firm.
9. Unmold onto chilled serving plate and, if desired, garnish with sprigs of parsley.

Dubonnet Chicken Salad Mold

ABOUT
10 SERVINGS

2 envelopes unflavored
   gelatin
1 cup cranberry juice
   cocktail
1 cup red Dubonnet
1 cup red currant syrup
1 envelope unflavored gelatin
¾ cup cold water
1 tablespoon soy sauce
1 cup mayonnaise
1½ cups finely diced cooked
   chicken
½ cup finely chopped celery
¼ cup toasted blanched
   almonds, finely chopped
½ cup whipping cream,
   whipped
Leaf lettuce
Cucumber slices, scored
Pitted ripe olives

1. Soften 2 envelopes gelatin in cranberry juice in a saucepan; set over low heat and stir until gelatin is dissolved. Remove from heat and stir in Dubonnet and currant syrup.
2. Pour into a 2-quart fancy tube mold. Chill until set but not firm.
3. Meanwhile, soften 1 envelope gelatin in cold water in a saucepan. Set over low heat and stir until gelatin is dissolved.
4. Remove from heat and stir in soy sauce and mayonnaise until thoroughly blended. Chill until mixture becomes slightly thicker. Mix in chicken, celery, and almonds. Fold in whipped cream until blended.
5. Spoon mixture into mold over first layer. Chill 8 hours or overnight.
6. Unmold onto a chilled serving plate. Garnish with lettuce, cucumber, and olives.

Chicken Salad

SERVES 4

1 cup diced cooked chicken
French dressing
2 tablespoons crushed,
   drained pineapple
1 cup diced celery
1 teaspoon grated onion
½ cup slivered, toasted
   almonds
Salad dressing

1. Marinate chicken in French dressing for 1 hour.
2. Drain. Add pineapple, celery, onion, almonds and salad dressing to moisten.
3. Season, if necessary. Chill.
4. Serve garnished with additional slivered almonds.

Chicken and Asparagus Salad
1½ cups diced cooked chicken, 1 cup asparagus tips, 2 tablespoons minced green pepper, ¼ cup shredded cabbage and ¾ cup mayonnaise.

Chicken and Bacon Salad
1 cup diced cooked chicken, ½ cup diced crisp bacon, 1 cup diced tomatoes and ½ cup mayonnaise or salad dressing.

Chicken and Cabbage Salad
½ cup diced cooked chicken, 2 cups shredded cabbage, ½ cup diced cooked ham and ¾ cup mayonnaise or salad dressing.

Chicken and Chestnut Salad
1 cup diced cooked chicken, ½ cup chopped cooked chestnuts, 1 cup diced celery, 2 hard-cooked eggs, chopped, ⅓ cup sliced stuffed olives and ½ cup mayonnaise or salad dressing.

Chicken and Cucumber Salad
2 cups diced cooked chicken, ½ cup chopped celery, ½ cup diced cucumbers, 2 tablespoons capers and ¾ cup mayonnaise or salad dressing.

Chicken and Orange Salad
2 cups diced cooked chicken, 2 oranges separated into

segments, ¼ teaspoon salt, 1 cup chopped celery, ½ cup chopped salted almonds and ¾ cup mayonnaise or salad dressing.

Chicken and Tongue Salad
1 cup diced cooked chicken, 1 cup diced cooked tongue, ½ cup chopped celery, ½ cup sliced stuffed olives and ¾ cup mayonnaise or salad dressing.

Chicken Livers in Madeira Sauce

4 SERVINGS

1 pound chicken livers
Milk
1 medium onion, minced
2 tablespoons chicken fat or butter
⅔ cup all-purpose flour
¾ teaspoon salt
⅔ cup chicken broth
½ cup Madeira

1. Cover chicken livers with milk; soak 2 hours. Drain; discard milk.
2. Sauté onion in fat.
3. Mix flour with salt. Coat livers with seasoned flour.
4. Add livers to onions. Stir-fry just until golden, about 5 minutes.
5. Stir in broth and wine. Cover. Simmer 5 to 10 minutes, or just until livers are tender.

Chicken Livers and Mushrooms

ABOUT
6 SERVINGS

2 pounds chicken livers, thawed if frozen
½ cup enriched all-purpose flour
1 teaspoon salt
¼ teaspoon ground white pepper
⅓ cup butter or margarine
1 cup orange sections, cut in halves
1 can (6 ounces) broiled mushrooms
Fresh parsley, snipped

1. Rinse chicken livers and drain on absorbent paper. Mix flour, salt, and peper; coat chicken livers evenly.
2. Heat butter in a large skillet, add chicken livers, and cook 10 minutes, or until livers are lightly browned and tender. Mix in orange sections; heat.
3. Meanwhile, heat mushrooms in their broth in a small skillet.
4. Arrange cooked chicken livers and heated orange sections on a hot platter. Top with mushrooms and sprinkle with parsley. Serve immediately.

Giblets with Rice

SERVES 6 TO 8

¼ cup butter or margarine
½ cup chopped onion
1 pound giblets (gizzard, heart and liver)
1½ teaspoons salt
4 medium carrots, sliced
1 teaspoon paprika
1 cup uncooked rice
3 tablespoons chopped parsley

1. Melt butter in a large saucepan.
2. Add onion and cook until lightly browned.
3. Rinse and trim any gristle from giblets.
4. Cut giblets into cubes; refrigerate liver.
5. Add gizzards, hearts and ½ teaspoon salt to saucepan; cover with water.
6. Simmer, covered, until tender.
7. Drain stock, adding enough water, if necessary, to make 3 cups.
8. Return to saucepan and bring to boiling.
9. Add carrots, paprika, and remaining salt.
10. Return to boiling and stir in the rice and livers.
11. Cover tightly and simmer about 25 minutes or until rice is tender and fluffy.
12. Stir in parsley and serve.

Rock Cornish Hens

Hens in Wine

4 SERVINGS

1 tablespoon rosemary
1 cup dry white wine
⅓ cup flour
1 teaspoon salt
½ teaspoon pepper
1 teaspoon snipped parsley
4 Rock Cornish hens, quartered
½ cup butter or margarine
1 pound small fresh mushrooms

1. Soak rosemary in wine 1 hour.
2. Combine flour, salt, pepper, and parsley. Coat hen quarters with flour mixture.
3. Brown hen quarters in butter in a skillet. Place in a 12x8-inch baking dish. Add wine mixture.
4. Bake, uncovered, at 350°F 30 minutes.
5. Meanwhile, sauté mushrooms in butter in skillet. Add to baking dish. Bake an additional 15 minutes, or until hen quarters are tender.

Game Hens with Spicy Stuffing

4 SERVINGS

3½ cups slightly dry bread cubes
½ cup chopped, drained sweet mixed pickles
½ cup diced dried figs
1 egg, slightly beaten
¼ teaspoon salt
⅛ teaspoon poultry seasoning
½ cup chopped celery
¼ cup butter or margarine
4 frozen Rock Cornish game hens (1 pound each), thawed
2 tablespoons butter or margarine, melted

1. Toss together lightly in a bowl the bread cubes, pickles, figs, egg, salt, and poultry seasoning.
2. Sauté celery in ¼ cup butter 1 minute. Toss with bread mixture. Spoon into cavities of hens; truss and arrange securely on a spit.
3. Roast hens on rotisserie about 1 hour, or until well browned and tender, brushing occasionally with melted butter.

Rock Cornish Hens with Fruited Stuffing

4 SERVINGS

1½ cups herb-seasoned stuffing croutons
½ cup drained canned apricot halves, cut in pieces
½ cup quartered seedless green grapes
⅓ cup chopped pecans
¼ cup butter or margarine, melted
2 tablespoons apricot nectar
1 tablespoon chopped parsley
¼ teaspoon salt
4 Rock Cornish hens (1 to 1½ pounds each), thawed if purchased frozen
Salt and pepper
⅓ cup apricot nectar
2 teaspoons soy sauce

1. Combine stuffing croutons, apricots, grapes, pecans, 2 tablespoons butter, 2 tablespoons apricot nectar, parsley, and ¼ teaspoon salt in a bowl; mix lightly.
2. Sprinkle cavities of hens with salt and pepper. Fill each hen with about ½ cup stuffing; fasten with skewers and lace with cord.
3. Blend ⅓ cup apricot nectar, soy sauce, and remaining butter. Place hens, breast side up, on a rack in a shallow roasting pan; brush generously with sauce.
4. Roast in a 350°F oven about 1½ hours, or until hens are tender and well browned; baste occasionally with sauce during roasting.

Cornish Hens with Raisin Stuffing

4 SERVINGS

4 Cornish hens (1 to 1½ pounds each)
16 grapevine leaves preserved in brine*
⅔ cup dark raisins
⅓ cup brandy
¾ cup cooked long-grain rice
1¼ cups finely chopped carrot
1¼ cups finely chopped celery
½ teaspoon cinnamon
1 tablespoon clarified butter
¼ teaspoon salt
⅛ teaspoon pepper
½ cup brandy

1. Rinse hens and pat dry; sprinkle lightly with salt.
2. Soak grapevine leaves in cold water 20 minutes. Pat dry. Set aside.
3. Simmer raisins in brandy 15 minutes; remove from heat and let stand 15 minutes. Stir in rice, carrot, celery, cinnamon, clarified butter, ¼ teaspoon salt, and the pepper. Spoon stuffing lightly into cavities of hens. Place hens on rack in a roasting pan. Cover breasts with grapevine leaves.
4. Roast in a 325°F oven 1¼ to 1½ hours, or until hens are tender. Baste with brandy during last ½ hour of roasting. Let hens stand 15 minutes before serving. Remove grapevine leaves.

*Grapevine leaves can be purchased in a gourmet shop or in the specialty department of a supermarket.

Spit-Roasted Cornish Hens

6 SERVINGS

3 Rock Cornish hens (1 pound each), at room temperature
Salt and peper
½ cup olive oil, salad oil, or butter
¼ cup lemon juice
1 teaspoon salt
1 teaspoon marjoram
1 teaspoon thyme
½ teaspoon pepper
1 clove garlic, minced
2 tablespoons chopped chives

1. Season cavity of each hen with salt and pepper. Close neck and abdominal openings with skewers. Tie wings to bodies and tie legs together. Put a spit fork on rod. Dovetail hens and put second spit fork on rod. Insert spit forks in hens. Tighten screws with pliers. Attach spit with hens to rotisserie.
2. Combine the remaining ingredients and mix well. Start motor and brush hens with sauce. Roast over medium coals, about 6 inches from heat, until leg joints move easily and meat pulls away from leg bones, about 1 hour; brush frequently with sauce.
3. Split hens into halves with poultry shears or a sharp knife.
Note: If using a gas-fired grill, sear hens for 2 minutes on high. Turn heat to medium and cook, brushing with sauce, until hens test done.

Roast Rock Cornish Hen
with Wild Rice and Mushrooms

4 TO 8
SERVINGS

1½ cups water
½ teaspoon salt
½ cup wild rice
2 tablespoons butter or
   margarine
½ pound mushrooms, sliced
   lengthwise through caps
   and stems
1 tablespoon finely chopped
   onion
3 tablespoons melted butter
   or margarine
2 tablespoons madeira
4 Rock Cornish hens, about
   1 pound each
2 teaspoons salt
¼ cup unsalted butter, melted
Watercress (optional)

1. Bring the water and salt to boiling in a deep saucepan.
2. Wash rice in a sieve. Add rice gradually to water so that boiling will not stop. Boil rapidly, covered, 30 to 40 minutes, or until a kernel of rice is entirely tender when pressed between fingers. Drain rice in a colander or sieve.
3. While rice is cooking, heat 2 tablespoons butter or margarine in a skillet. Add the mushrooms and onion; cook, stirring occasionally, until mushrooms are lightly browned. Conbine mushrooms, wild rice, melted butter, and madeira; toss gently until mushrooms and butter are evenly distributed throughout rice.
4. Rinse and pat hens with absorbent paper. Rub cavities of the hens with the salt. Lightly fill body cavities with the wild rice stuffing. To close body cavities, sew or skewer and lace with cord. Fasten neck skin to backs and wings to bodies with skewers.
5. Place hens, breast-side up, on rack in roasting pan. Brush each hen with melted unsalted butter (about 1 tablespoon).
6. Roast, uncovered, in a 350°F oven; frequently baste hens during roasting period with drippings from roasting pan. Roast 1 to 1½ hours, or until hens test done. To test, move leg gently by grasping end bone; drumstick-thigh joint moves easily when hens are done. Remove skewers, if used.
7. Transfer hens to a heated serving platter and garnish with sprigs of watercress if desired.

Rock Cornish Hens with Oranges
and Almonds

1 Rock Cornish hen per
   serving

For each serving:
2 tablespoons butter, melted
2 tablespoons orange juice
Salt and pepper to taste
¼ teaspoon marjoram
¼ teaspoon thyme
½ garlic clove, crushed in a
   garlic press
½ navel orange with peel,
   cut in thin slices
2 tablespoons honey (about)
5 almonds, blanched,
   slivered, and toasted

1. Rinse hen well. Drain and pat dry. Place in a shallow baking dish. Drizzle inside and out with butter.
2. Combine orange juice, salt, pepper, marjoram, thyme, and garlic in a small bowl. Pour over and into the bird. Marinate 2 hours; turn occasionally.
3. Set bird on a broiler rack and put under broiler about 6 inches from heat. Broil 12 minutes on each side, or until tender, basting frequently with the marinade. During the last few minutes of broiling, arrange orange slices around the bird and drizzle with honey.
4. Garnish with almonds and serve at once.

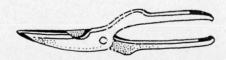

Turkeys

Timed to come to market all year round, whole turkeys are available *dressed* (birds that have been bled and feather-dressed but have head, feet and viscera intact) or *ready-to-cook,* fully cleaned and ready for cooking. Today almost all turkeys are completely eviscerated, vacuum-sealed in sturdy plastic bags which eliminate air pockets (and thus freezer burn), then quick-frozen and held at 0° F. from processing plant to the consumer. Ready-to-cook turkeys are sold fresh or ice-chilled in a few markets, but as a rule are not easily obtainable.

Roast Turkey I

ABOUT
16 SERVINGS

1 ready-to-cook turkey (10 to 12 pounds)
Oyster Stuffing
Salt
Melted fat
Gravy (favorite recipe)

1. Rinse bird with cold water. Drain and pat dry with absorbent paper or soft cloth.
2. Prepare oyster stuffing.
3. Rub body and neck cavities with salt. Fill lightly with stuffing. (Extra stuffing may be put into a greased covered baking dish or wrapped in aluminum foil and baked with turkey the last half hour of roasting time.)
4. Fasten neck skin to back with skewer and bring wing tips onto back. Push drumsticks under band of skin at tail, or tie with cord. Set, breast up, on rack in shallow roasting pan. Brush with melted fat.
5. If meat thermometer is used, insert it in center of inside thigh muscle or thickest part of breast meat. Be sure that

(continued)

tip does not touch bones. If desired, cover top and sides of turkey with cheesecloth moistened with melted fat. Keep cloth moist during roasting by brushing occasionally with fat from bottom of pan.

6. Roast, uncovered, at 325°F 4 to 4½ hours. When turkey is two-thirds done, cut band of skin or cord at drumsticks. Continue roasting until turkey tests done (the thickest part of the drumstick feels soft when pressed with fingers and meat thermometer registers 180° to 185°F).

7. For easier carving, let turkey stand 20 to 30 minutes, keeping it warm. Meanwhile, prepare gravy from drippings.

8. Remove cord and skewers from turkey and place on heated platter. Garnish platter as desired.

Oyster Stuffing: Combine **3 quarts soft bread crumbs, 4 teaspoons salt,** ½ **teaspoon pepper, 1 pint to 1 quart small oysters,** whole or cut in small pieces, **¾ cup oyster liquor** (use turkey stock or milk if needed), ½ **cup butter** or **turkey fat,** melted, mixing well.

Roast Turkey II (Pictured on page 55)

ABOUT
16 SERVINGS

1 turkey, 10 to 12 pounds, ready-to-cook weight
Oyster Stuffing (above)
2 teaspoons salt
Melted fat

1. Set out a shallow roasting pan with rack.
2. Clean turkey (and cut off neck at body, leaving skin).
3. (If turkey is frozen, thaw according to directions on package.) Rinse, drain and pat turkey with absorbent paper. Set aside.
4. Prepare Oyster Stuffing.
5. Rub cavities of turkey with salt.
6. Lightly fill body and neck cavities with stuffing. To close body cavity, sew or skewer and lace with cord. Fasten neck skin to back with skewer. Tie drumsticks to tail. Bring wing tips onto back. Brush skin thoroughly with melted fat.
7. Place breast up on rack in roasting pan.
8. If roast meat thermometer is used, place it in center of inside thigh muscle. When done, roast meat thermometer will register 190°F. Place fat-moistened cheesecloth over top and sides of turkey. Keep cloth moist during roasting by brushing occasionally with fat from bottom of pan.
9. Roast uncovered at 325°F 4 to 4½ hours, or until turkey tests done (thickest part of drumstick feels soft when pressed with fingers. Protect fingers with cloth or paper napkin.) Remove turkey from oven. Remove roast meat thermometer and keep turkey hot. Allow to stand about 20 minutes before serving. This makes it easier to carve the turkey and also allows time for last-minute preparations such as preparing gravy and garnishes.
10. Remove cord and skewers. Serve turkey on heated platter. Garnish with **parsley** and serve with **cranberry sauce.** If desired, put **paper frills** on drumsticks.

Roast Half Turkey: Follow recipe for Roast Turkey. Use half or quarter turkey, 3½ to 5 pounds, ready-to-cook weight. Rub cut side with one half salt mixture. Skewer skin

along cut sides to prevent shrinking. Tie leg to tail and wing flat against breast. Place skin-side up on rack. Roast at 325°F about 2 hours. Meanwhile, prepare **stuffing for half turkey.** Remove turkey from rack. Spoon stuffing onto a piece of aluminum foil and place on rack. Cover stuffing with half turkey. Roast 1 to 1½ hours longer, or until thickest part of drumstick feels soft when pressed with fingers. (Protect fingers with cloth or paper napkin.)
ABOUT 8 SERVINGS

Roast Turkey III

1 ready-to-cook turkey
  (reserve giblets)
1 lime, halved
1 orange, halved
Salt and freshly ground
  pepper
¼ cup olive oil
1 tablespoon tomato paste
1 garlic clove, crushed in a
  garlic press
1 quart water
1 large onion, sliced
4 parsley sprigs
1 bay leaf
2 teaspoons salt
Lettuce
Cherry tomato
Avocado half
Green pepper ring
2 tablespoons butter
2 tablespoons cornstarch

1. Rub the skin of the bird with the cut side of the lime and orange. Sprinkle salt and pepper over surface. Refrigerate 2 hours.
2. Combine oil, tomato paste, and garlic. Brush mixture over bird. Set on a rack in a shallow roasting pan.
3. Roast, uncovered, in a 375°F oven until turkey tests done (the thickest part of the drumstick feels soft when pressed with fingers, or meat thermometer inserted in the thickest part of inner thigh muscle registers 180°F to 185°F).
4. Meanwhile, prepare giblet broth. Put turkey neck and giblets (except liver), water, onion, parsley, bay leaf, and salt in a saucepan. Cover and simmer about 2 hours, or until giblets are tender. Add the liver the last 15 minutes of cooking. Strain.
5. Carve turkey and arrange meat on a bed of lettuce. Garnish with tomato, avocado, and green pepper.
6. Remove excess fat from roasting pan. Pour in 2 cups giblet broth to deglaze over medium heat.
7. Mix butter and cornstarch and add to broth. Stir until sauce is slightly thicker.
8. Serve sauce with turkey.

Roast Turkey with Anchovies

12 TO 18
SERVINGS

1 turkey (12 to 15 pounds)
5 slices bacon
1 large onion, minced
¾ pound veal (2 cups
  ground)
3 slices stale bread, cubed
⅓ cup milk or chicken broth
1 can (2 ounces) flat
  anchovies
2 tablespoons butter
2 eggs, beaten
Grated peel and juice of 1
  lemon
½ teaspoon pepper
⅔ cup melted butter

1. Rinse turkey with running water. Dry with paper towels.
2. Dice bacon. Fry until transparent. Add onion; stir-fry until golden. Stir in veal, bread cubes, and milk. Remove from heat.
3. Finely chop or mash anchovies. Mix in butter, lemon peel and juice, and pepper; beat until well combined. Add to meat mixture and stir until well blended. Stuffing should be of a paste consistency.
4. Spread stuffing in cavity of turkey. Truss.
5. Place turkey in roasting pan. If desired, insert meat thermometer in thickest part of breast.
6. Roast at 425°F about 3½ hours, basting frequently with melted butter and pan drippings. When done, leg of turkey moves easily and meat thermometer registers 180° to 185°F.

Stuffed Turkey

12 TO 16
SERVINGS

1 turkey (12 to 16 pounds)
Salt and pepper
Juice of 1 lemon
Stuffing (see below)
Melted butter

Gravy:
Flour
Chicken broth
White wine
Salt and pepper

1. Clean turkey. Sprinkle inside and out with salt and pepper, then drizzle with lemon juice.
2. Spoon desired amount of stuffing into cavities of turkey. Secure openings with skewers and twine.
3. Put turkey, breast side up, on a rack in a shallow roasting pan. Cover bird with a double thickness of cheesecloth soaked in butter.
4. Roast in a 325°F oven 4½ to 5½ hours, or until done (180°F to 185°F on a meat thermometer inserted in inside thigh muscle or thickest part of breast); baste with drippings several times during roasting.
5. For gravy, stir a small amount of flour with pan drippings. Cook until bubbly. Stir in equal parts of broth and wine. Season to taste with salt and pepper.
6. Put turkey on a platter and garnish with **watercress**. Accompany with gravy.

Stuffing

5 slices bacon, diced
1 onion, chopped
1 clove garlic, minced
3 pounds ground pork loin
½ cup tomato purée
¾ cup blanched almonds, chopped
½ cup ripe olives, coarsely chopped
6 jalapeño chilies, seeded and chopped
3 carrots, pared and sliced
3 bananas, peeled and sliced
3 apples, pared, cored, and diced
¾ cup raisins
2 teaspoons sugar
Salt and pepper
Cinnamon

1. Fry bacon until brown in a large skillet. Remove bacon from fat; reserve. Brown onion and garlic in fat in skillet, then brown meat. Discard excess fat.
2. Add tomato purée, almonds, olives, chilies, carrots, fruit, sugar, and salt, pepper, and cinnamon to taste; mix well. Cook several minutes. Mix in bacon. Cool before stuffing turkey.

Roast Stuffed Turkey

6 TO 8
SERVINGS

1 turkey (6 to 8 pounds)
1 package (7 ounces) herb-seasoned stuffing croutons
½ cup melted butter
½ cup hot water or chicken broth
2 tablespoons butter
½ cup chopped celery
½ cup chopped onion
2 tablespoons chopped parsley
Melted butter

1. Rinse turkey with cold water; pat dry.
2. Turn stuffing croutons into a bowl; add ½ cup melted butter and toss gently. Stir in hot water or broth.
3. Heat 2 tablespoons butter in a skillet. Add celery and onion; cook until tender. Add to bowl with stuffing; add parsley and toss to mix.
4. Spoon stuffing into cavities of bird. Place turkey, breast side up, in a large electric cooker. Insert a meat thermometer in inner thigh muscle. Brush with melted butter.
5. Cover and roast at 300°F until meat thermometer registers 180° to 185°F, about 6 hours.

Note: If desired to enhance browning, place a piece of aluminum foil over turkey before covering with lid.

Roast Turkey (page 52)

Stuffing for a Small Turkey

STUFFING FOR
A SMALL
TURKEY OR
2 CAPONS

½ cup butter
1 onion, minced
1 medium cooking apple,
  pared, cored and diced
1 pound mushrooms, sliced
2 medium potatoes, boiled,
  peeled, and diced
½ cup pine nuts
½ cup dried black currants
1 cup blanched almonds,
  sliced
2 pounds chestnuts, boiled
  and cleaned
4 cups prepared bread
  stuffing
2 cups or more chicken stock
  to make a moist stuffing
1 can (4½ ounces) pâté de
  foie gras
Salt and pepper to taste

1. Melt butter in a large deep skillet. Add onion, apple, and mushrooms; cook until tender.
2. Add potatoes, pine nuts, currants, almonds, chestnuts, stuffing, and stock. Heat thoroughly over low heat, adding more liquid if necessary.
3. Stir in pâté. Season with salt and pepper.
4. Cool completely. Stuff bird.

Roast Turkey with Herbed Stuffing

ABOUT
25 SERVINGS

Cooked Giblets and Broth
4 quarts ½-inch enriched
  bread cubes
1 cup snipped parsley
2 to 2½ teaspoons salt
2 teaspoons thyme
2 teaspoons rosemary,
  crushed
2 teaspoons marjoram
1 teaspoon ground sage
1 cup butter or margarine
1 cup coarsely chopped
  onion
1 cup coarsely chopped
  celery with leaves
1 turkey (14 to 15 pounds)
Fat
3 tablespoons flour
¼ teaspoon salt
⅛ teaspoon ground black
  pepper

1. Prepare Cooked Giblets and Broth. Measure 1 cup chopped cooked giblets; set the broth aside.
2. Combine bread cubes, reserved giblets, and parsley in a large bowl. Blend salt, thyme, rosemary, marjoram, and sage; add to bread mixture and toss to mix.
3. Heat butter in a skillet. Mix in onion and celery; cook about 5 minutes, stirring occasionally. Toss with the bread mixture.
4. Add 1 to 2 cups broth (depending upon how moist a stuffing is desired), mixing lightly until ingredients are thoroughly blended.
5. Rinse turkey with cold water; pat dry, inside and out, with absorbent paper. Lightly fill body and neck cavities with the stuffing. Fasten neck skin to back with a skewer. Bring wing tips onto back of bird. Push drumsticks under band of skin at tail, if present, or tie to tail with cord.
6. Place turkey, breast side up, on rack in a shallow roasting pan. Brush skin with fat. Insert meat thermometer in the thickest part of the inner thigh muscle, being sure that tip does not touch bone.
7. Roast in a 325°F oven about 5 hours, or until thermometer registers 180°F to 185°F. If desired, baste or brush bird occasionally with pan drippings. Place turkey on a heated platter; for easier carving, allow turkey to stand about 30 minutes.
8. Meanwhile, leaving brown residue in roasting pan, pour remaining drippings and fat into a bowl. Allow fat to rise to surface; skim off fat and measure 3 tablespoons into roasting pan. Blend flour, salt, and pepper with fat. Cook and stir until bubbly. Continue to stir while slowly adding 2 cups reserved liquid (broth and drippings). Cook, stirring

constantly, until gravy thickens; scrape pan to blend in brown residue. Cook 1 to 2 minutes. If desired, mix in finely chopped cooked giblets the last few minutes of cooking.

Cooked Giblets and Broth: Put **turkey neck** and **giblets** (except liver) into a saucepan with **1 large onion,** sliced, **parsley, celery with leaves, 1 medium bay leaf, 2 teaspoons salt,** and **1 cup water.** Cover, bring to boiling, reduce heat, and simmer until giblets are tender (about 2 hours); add the liver the last 15 minutes of cooking. Strain through a colander or sieve; reserve broth for stuffing. Chop giblets; set aside for stuffing and gravy.

Roast Turkey with Pineapple-Stuffed Breast

ABOUT 16 SERVINGS

1 turkey (10 to 12 pounds)
1½ tablespoons curry powder
2 teaspoons salt
⅓ cup minced onion
4 garlic cloves, minced
1 teaspoon minced ginger root
2 tablespoons vegetable oil
⅔ cup unsweetened pineapple juice
1 can (20 ounces) unsweetened crushed pineapple, drained
1½ cups minced cooked turkey or chicken
Unsweetened pineapple juice

1. Rinse turkey; pat dry. Carefully loosen skin over turkey breast by running fingers under the skin.
2. Mix curry powder; salt, onion, garlic, ginger root, vegetable oil, and ⅔ cup pineapple juice. Mix one quarter of the spice mixture with the drained pineapple and minced turkey. Spread pineapple mixture gently and evenly under skin of turkey breast with fingers. Place turkey in a roasting pan. Insert meat thermometer in thickest part of thigh. Brush remaining spice mixture over turkey breast.
3. Roast in a 325°F oven until thermometer registers 175°F (3½ to 4 hours); baste occasionally with pineapple juice. Remove turkey to serving platter; cover loosely with aluminum foil. Let stand 20 minutes before carving.

Note: This recipe can be used for a roasting chicken of about 5 pounds. Use half the spice and pineapple mixtures; proceed as directed. Roast at 325°F about 2½ hours, or until chicken is tender; drumstick meat will feel very soft.

Turkey Pot Pie

6 SERVINGS

2 cups chopped cooked turkey
2 cans (10¾ ounces each) condensed cream of celery soup
½ cup milk
½ teaspoon Worcestershire sauce
Dash pepper
6 cooked small onions
1 cup cooked cubed potato
1 cup cooked sliced carrot
⅓ cup shortening
1 cup self-rising flour
4 tablespoons cold water

1. Combine turkey, soup, milk, Worcestershire sauce, pepper, onions, potato, and carrot. Put into a 2-quart casserole.
2. Cut shortening into flour. Add water, a tablespoon at a time, mixing lightly until dough can be formed into a ball. (If necessary, add a little more water to make dough hold together.) Let rest 5 minutes.
3. Roll dough out on a lightly floured board or canvas to fit top of casserole. Cut slits to allow steam to escape. Adjust over filling; flute edges.
4. Bake, uncovered, at 425°F 20 minutes, or until pastry is golden brown.

Turkey 'n' Dressing Bake

6 SERVINGS

3 tablespoons butter or margarine
½ cup diced celery
¼ cup minced onion
3¼ cups chicken broth (dissolve 4 chicken bouillon cubes in 3¼ cups boiling water)
5 cups coarse whole wheat bread crumbs; reserve ½ cup crumbs for topping
¼ cup snipped parsley
½ teaspoon salt
¼ teaspoon ground black pepper
1 egg, slightly beaten
2 tablespoons flour
2 eggs, beaten
⅛ teaspoon ground black pepper
¼ teaspoon crushed leaf sage
¼ teaspoon celery salt
Thin slices of cooked turkey roast (see Note)
1 tablespoon butter or margarine, melted
Parsley, snipped

1. Heat 3 tablespoons butter in a large skillet. Mix in celery and onion and cook about 5 minutes. Combine vegetables with 1¾ cups chicken broth, 4½ cups bread crumbs, ¼ cup parsley, salt, ¼ teaspoon pepper, and 1 egg. Mix lightly with a fork. Spoon the mixture over bottom of a shallow 2-quart baking dish; set aside.
2. Mix flour and ¼ cup cool broth in a saucepan until smooth; heat until bubbly. Add remaining broth gradually, stirring constantly. Cook and stir over medium heat until sauce comes to boiling; cook 2 minutes. Remove from heat and gradually add to eggs while beating. Blend in remaining pepper, sage, and celery salt.
3. Arrange the desired amount of turkey over dressing in baking dish. Pour the sauce over all.
4. Toss reserved bread crumbs with melted butter; spoon over top.
5. Bake at 350°F 30 to 40 minutes, or until egg mixture is set. Garnish generously with parsley.

Note: Prepare frozen boneless turkey roast, following package directions.

Turkey Croquettes

2 tablespoons butter
2 tablespoons minced shallot
1½ tablespoons flour
½ cup chicken broth
2 egg yolks, beaten
2 cups ground turkey
1 tablespoon chopped parsley
1 teaspoon salt
¼ teaspoon freshly ground pepper
2 egg yolks
2 teaspoons cooking oil
Dry bread crumbs
Fat for deep frying, heated to 375°F

1. Melt butter in a skillet. Cook shallot over low heat until translucent. Stir in flour. Gradually add chicken broth, blending until smooth.
2. Remove from heat and beat 2 egg yolks. Add turkey, parsley, salt, and pepper; mix well.
3. Spread mixture on a platter and cool in refrigerator.
4. Shape mixture into small balls. Coat balls with a mixture of 2 egg yolks and oil and then roll in bread crumbs.
5. Fry in heated fat until golden. Drain on absorbent paper.
6. Serve with Tomato Sauce Creole (page 75).

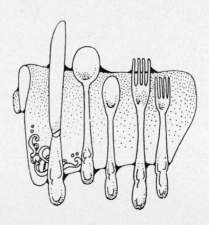

Ducklings

Duck with Red Cabbage

ABOUT
4 SERVINGS

1 head red cabbage,
  shredded
1 onion, chopped
Salt
6 ounces salt pork, diced
½ cup red wine or chicken
  broth
1 duck (5 to 6 pounds)

1. Put cabbage and onion in a bowl, sprinkle with salt, and let stand 10 minutes. Squeeze out liquid.
2. Fry salt pork in a skillet until golden. Add cabbage-onion mixture and wine. Cover and simmer 20 minutes.
3. Place duck in a roasting pan.
4. Bake at 425°F 30 minutes. Drain off fat. Spoon cabbage mixture over duck. Reduce oven temperature to 350°F. Bake about 45 minutes, or until duck is tender. Baste frequently.

Ducklings with Green Peppercorn Sauce

6 TO 8
SERVINGS

2 ducklings (about 4½
  pounds each)
1½ teaspoons salt
¼ teaspoon freshly ground
  pepper
1 teaspoon snipped fresh or
  ½ teaspoon dried crumbled
  rosemary leaves
Chicken Stock (page 74)
Green Peppercorn Sauce
  (page 75)

1. Rinse ducklings; pat dry. Place ducklings breast side up on rack in a roasting pan. Sprinkle with salt, pepper, and rosemary. Pierce breasts of ducklings with a fork several times.
2. Roast in a 350°F oven about 2½ hours, or until ducklings are done; drumstick meat will feel very tender. Baste ducklings occasionally with stock. Remove ducklings to a serving platter; let stand 15 minutes before carving.
3. Serve with the sauce.

Smothered Duck in Caper Sauce

ABOUT
4 SERVINGS

1 duck (5 to 6 pounds), cut
  up
1 clove garlic, crushed
  (optional)
Salt and pepper
3 tablespoons butter or
  bacon drippings
1 cup chicken or beef
  bouillon
2 tablespoons water
2 teaspoons cornstarch
⅓ cup capers
2 teaspoons brown or
  caramelized sugar
1 tablespoon lemon juice

1. Rub duck with garlic. Sprinkle cavity with salt and pepper to taste. Let stand 1 to 2 hours.
2. Melt butter in a heavy skillet or Dutch oven. Add duck and brown quickly on all sides. Drain off fat, if desired.
3. Add bouillon. Cover. Simmer over medium heat about 1 hour, or until duck is tender.
4. Remove duck to a heated platter.
5. Blend water into cornstarch. Stir into hot liquid in Dutch oven. Add capers, cook and stir over high heat until sauce boils. Reduce heat. Add sugar and lemon juice. Stir just until sauce is thickened.

Crumb-Crusted Duckling Halves

Crumb-Crusted Duckling Halves

4 SERVINGS

16 grapevine leaves pre-
served in brine*
2 ducklings (about 4½
pounds each), cut in half
2 teaspoons salt
½ cup Chicken Stock
(page #)
Juice of 1 lemon
Clarified butter
⅓ cup seasoned stuffing
crumbs, slightly crushed
Cumberland Sauce (page 75)
or Madeira Sauce (page 75)

1. Soak grapevine leaves in cold water 20 minutes. Pat dry. Set aside.
2. Using fingers and a sharp knife, remove skin and excess fat from ducklings (do not skin wings). Place ducklings breast side up on rack in a roasting pan; sprinkle with salt. Cover surface of ducks with grapevine leaves.
3. Roast in a 325°F oven about 2½ hours, or until ducklings are done; drumstick meat will feel soft. Baste ducklings every half hour with a mixture of stock and lemon juice.
4. Remove grapevine leaves. Brush ducklings very lightly with butter and sprinkle with crumbs. Broil 4 inches from heat until crumbs are browned (about 5 minutes). Remove ducklings to platter; let stand 10 minutes before serving. Serve with desired sauce.

*Grapevine leaves can be purchased in a gourmet shop or in the specialty section of a supermarket.

Duck Bigarade (Pictured on page 63)

4 SERVINGS

2 limes, halved
1 ready-to-cook duck (about
5 pounds)
Salt, freshly ground pepper,
and cayenne or red pepper
2 cups firmly packed brown sugar
1 cup water
2 teaspoons vanilla extract
½ cup orange peel strips
4 small oranges, halved and seeded
2 cups chicken broth
¼ cup orange juice
½ cup amber rum
¼ cup butter
¼ cup cornstarch

1. Squeeze lime juice over the entire duck. Season with salt, pepper, and cayenne. Place on a rack in a roasting pan.
2. Roast, uncovered in a 425°F oven 25 minutes. Turn oven control to 350°F and continue to roast 30 minutes.
3. Combine brown sugar, water, and vanilla extract in a large, heavy saucepan. Bring to a boil over high heat and boil about 6 minutes. Add orange peel and orange halves and continue boiling 1 minute. Remove from heat and cool. Set ¼ cup syrup aside in a small saucepan.
4. Transfer duck to a warm platter. Remove fat from roasting pan. Stir in chicken broth and orange juice to deglaze. Heat the rum, ignite it, and when flames die down, pour it into the chicken broth.

5. Heat the reserved syrup until it caramelizes. Add to chicken broth mixture and blend well.

6. Mix butter and cornstarch and add to roasting pan. Cook over medium heat, stirring constantly, until the gravy is slightly thicker.

7. Carve the duck. Sprinkle the glazed orange peel strips over the meat. Pour a little gravy over the meat. Serve remaining gravy separately. Arrange glazed orange halves around the duck, alternating with bouquets of **watercress**. Serve with Caribbean Rice (page 77) .

Duckling with Fruit Salad

6 SERVINGS

2 ducklings (about 4½ pounds each)
2 teaspoons salt
½ teaspoon freshly ground pepper
¾ teaspoon allspice
½ cup fruit juice
6 slices fresh or canned pineapple
6 preserved kumquats, thinly sliced
3 oranges, peeled and segments removed
2 apples, sliced
2 papayas, peeled and sliced, if desired
2 bananas, sliced
1 pound white grapes
1 lime, cut in 6 wedges
1 lemon, cut in 6 wedges
1½ cups Low-Fat Yogurt
2 tablespoons snipped mint
Mint sprigs

1. Rinse ducklings; pat dry. Place ducklings breast side up on rack in a roasting pan. Sprinkle with salt, pepper, and allspice. Pierce breasts of ducklings with a fork several times.

2. Roast in a 350°F oven about 2½ hours, or until ducklings are done; drumstick meat will feel very soft. Baste ducklings occasionally with fruit juice. Remove ducklings to platter; let cool.

3. While ducklings are roasting, prepare fruits; refrigerate. Mix yogurt and snipped mint; refrigerate.

4. Carefully cut skin and fat from ducklings. Remove meat from carcass carefully, keeping meat in as large pieces as possible. Arrange duckling meat and fruits attractively on individual plates. Garnish with mint. Pass chilled yogurt sauce.

Curried Duck Martinique

6 SERVINGS

3 cups coarsely chopped cooked duck
3 cups sliced mushrooms
6 tablespoons butter, melted
1 cup diced apple
⅓ cup grated onion
1 garlic clove, crushed in a garlic press
3 tablespoons flour
1 tablespoon curry powder
½ teaspoon salt
¼ teaspoon freshly ground pepper
1 cup whipping cream
½ cup duck stock (made from cooking the carcass)
3 tablespoons Madeira or sweet sherry

1. Cook duck and mushrooms in half the melted butter in a skillet over low heat, until the duck is slightly browned and the mushrooms are tender. Remove from heat and cover.

2. Sauté apple, onion, and garlic in remaining butter in a large skillet until soft. Remove skillet from the heat and stir in flour, curry, salt, and pepper.

3. Place skillet over low heat and blend in cream, stock, and Madeira. Stir constantly until the mixture thickens. Stir in the duck and mushroom mixture.

4. Serve with **cooked white rice** tossed with 1 cup diced banana.

Glazed Duckling Gourmet

6 TO 8
SERVINGS

2 ducklings (about 4 pounds
  each), quartered (do not
  use wings, necks, and
  backs) and skinned
1½ teaspoons salt
¼ teaspoon ground nutmeg
3 to 4 tablespoons butter
1 clove garlic, minced
1½ teaspoons rosemary,
  crushed
1½ teaspoons thyme
1½ cups burgundy
2 teaspoons red wine vinegar
⅓ cup currant jelly
2 teaspoons cornstarch
2 tablespoons cold water
1½ cups halved seedless
  green grapes
Watercress

1. Remove excess fat from duckling pieces; rinse duckling and pat dry with absorbent paper. Rub pieces with salt and nutmeg.
2. Heat butter and garlic in a large skillet over medium heat; add the duckling pieces and brown well on all sides.
3. Add rosemary, thyme, burgundy, vinegar, and jelly to skillet. Bring to boiling; cover and simmer over low heat until duckling is tender (about 45 minutes). Remove duckling to a heated platter and keep it warm.
4. Combine cornstarch and water; blend into liquid in skillet; bring to boiling and cook 1 to 2 minutes, stirring constantly. Add grapes and toss them lightly until thoroughly heated.
5. Pour the hot sauce over duckling; garnish platter with watercress.

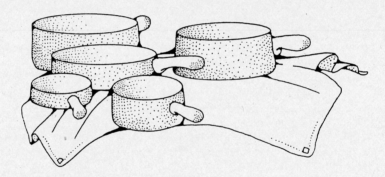

Roast Duckling with Olives

4 SERVINGS

1 duckling (about 4 pounds)
⅓ cup olive oil or other
  cooking oil
2 medium carrots, coarsely
  chopped
1 large onion, coarsely
  chopped
½ teaspoon salt
⅛ teaspoon seasoned pepper
¼ teaspoon rosemary
⅛ teaspoon savory
2 small stalks celery,
  chopped
3 sprigs parsley, chopped
1 small bay leaf
⅓ cup cognac
2 tablespoons tomato paste
2 cups hot chicken broth or
  bouillon
⅓ cup dry white wine
16 whole pitted green olives

1. Rinse, pat dry, and cut duckling into quarters. Remove any excess fat from pieces.
2. Heat oil in skillet; add duckling pieces and cook over medium heat until well browned on all sides. Remove pieces from skillet and keep warm.
3. Add carrots, onion, salt, seasoned pepper, rosemary, savory, celery, parsley, and bay leaf to skillet; continue cooking until carrots and onions are lightly browned. Drain off excess fat in skillet.
4. Return duck to skillet and pour cognac over it. Ignite and when flame ceases add a blend of tomato paste, chicken broth, and white wine. Cover skillet and cook in a 350°F oven about 1½ hours, or until duckling is tender.
5. Remove to heated serving platter and keep warm. Strain remaining mixture in skillet into a saucepan and add green olives. Heat until sauce is very hot and pour over duckling.

Duck Bigarade (page 60)

Canard à l'Orange

8 SERVINGS

2 ducklings (4 to 5 pounds each)
2 teaspoons salt
½ teaspoon pepper
1 clove garlic, peeled and cut crosswise into halves
½ cup dry white wine
½ cup orange marmalade

Sauce:
2 tablespoons butter or margarine
1 can (13¾ ounces) condensed chicken broth
½ cup orange marmalade
¼ cup dry white wine
¼ cup orange juice
2 teaspoons cornstarch
2 teaspoons lemon juice
2 tablespoons slivered orange peel

1. If frozen, let ducklings thaw according to package directions. Remove giblets, necks, and livers from ducklings. Reserve livers for sauce; if desired, reserve giblets and necks for soup stock. Remove and discard excess fat. Wash, drain, and pat dry with paper toweling. Rub cavities with salt, pepper, and garlic. Fasten neck skin to back with a skewer. Tuck tail ends into cavities. Tie legs together and tuck wing tips under ducklings. Prick skin generously to release fat. Place ducklings, breast side up, on a rack in a large shallow roasting pan.

2. Roast at 350°F 2 to 2½ hours or until legs can be moved easily, basting several times during roasting and removing accumulated drippings about every 30 minutes. Remove ducklings from oven and spread surface with mixture of wine and marmalade. Return to oven and continue roasting for 10 minutes.

3. For sauce, melt butter in a skillet. Add duckling livers and sauté until lightly browned. Remove and chop livers. Add chicken broth, marmalade, wine, orange juice, and cornstarch blended with lemon juice. Cook, stirring constantly over low heat for 10 minutes or until sauce bubbles and thickens. Stir in chopped livers and orange peel.

4. Transfer ducklings to a heated platter. Remove skewers and twine. Garnish, if desired, with watercress and orange slices. Reheat sauce if necessary and serve with duckling.

Geese

Goose is sweet-meated (all dark meat), tender and juicy. Label information in individual packaged goose should be relied upon in selecting the bird, now available in two classes: young goose (about 4 to 8 pounds), which is tender-meated, and mature goose (up to 14 pounds). Market styles are: ready-to-cook (either fresh or quick-frozen) or dressed. About 1 pound per serving is a good allowance in choosing size or quantity.

Stuffings that have little or no added fat are usually preferred. Celery, onion, apple, cranberry, dried fruit stuffings (apricot, currants, prunes, raisins), sauerkraut and mashed potato are among the favorites.

Thaw goose if frozen. Rinse body cavity with cold water, removing any bits of lung, etc. Any large fat layers also should be removed from body cavity. Pat dry. Abdominal opening should be closed with cord and skewers.

Roast Goose with Rice-and-Pickle Stuffing

6 TO 8 SERVINGS

3 cups cooked rice; or 1 package (6 ounces) seasoned white and wild rice mix, cooked following package directions
1 package (7 ounces) herb-seasoned stuffing croutons
2 medium navel oranges, pared and sectioned
2 onions, chopped
1 cup cranberries, rinsed, sorted, and chopped
1 cup sweet mixed pickles, drained and chopped
¼ cup sweet pickle liquid
½ to ¾ cup butter or margarine, melted
2 tablespoons brown sugar
1 goose (8 to 10 pounds)
1 tablespoon salt
¼ teaspoon ground black pepper
2 tablespoons light corn syrup
1½ cups orange juice
½ cup orange marmalade

1. Combine rice, stuffing croutons, orange sections, onions, cranberries, pickles and liquid, butter, and brown sugar in a large bowl; toss lightly until blended.
2. Rinse goose and remove any large layers of fat from the body cavity. Pat dry with absorbent paper. Rub body and neck cavities with salt and pepper.
3. Lightly spoon stuffing into the neck and body cavities. Overlap neck cavity with the skin and skewer to back of goose. Close body cavity with skewers and lace with cord. Loop cord around legs; tighten slightly and tie to a skewer inserted in the back above tail. Rub skin of goose with a little salt, if desired.
4. Put remaining stuffing into a greased casserole and cover; or cook in heavy-duty aluminum foil. Set in oven with goose during final hour of roasting.
5. Place goose, breast side down, on a rack in a large shallow roasting pan.
6. Roast in a 325°F oven 2 hours, removing fat from pan several times during this period.
7. Turn goose, breast side up. Blend corn syrup and 1 cup orange juice. Brush generously over goose. Roast about 1½ hours, or until goose tests done. To test for doneness, move leg gently by grasping end of bone; when done, drumstick-thigh joint moves easily or twists out. Brush frequently during final roasting period with the orange-syrup blend.
8. Transfer goose to a heated serving platter. Spoon 2 tablespoons drippings, the remaining ½ cup orange juice, and marmalade into a small saucepan. Heat thoroughly, stirring to blend. Pour into a serving dish or gravy boat to accompany goose.

Roast Goose with Prune-Apple Stuffing

8 SERVINGS

2 cups pitted cooked prunes
1 goose (10 to 12 pounds,
    ready-to-cook weight)
Salt
6 medium (about 2 pounds)
    apples

1. Set out a shallow roasting pan with rack. Have prunes ready, reserving about 8 to 10 prunes for garnish.
2. If goose is frozen, thaw according to directions on package. Clean and remove any layers of fat from body cavity and opening of goose. Cut off neck at body, leaving on neck skin. Rinse and pat dry with absorbent paper. (Reserve giblets for use in gravy or other food preparation.) Rub body and neck cavities of goose with salt. Wash, core, pare and quarter apples.
3. Lightly fill body and neck cavities with the apples and prunes. To close body cavity, sew or skewer and lace with cord. Fasten neck skin to back with skewer. Loop cord around legs and tighten slightly. Place breast side down on rack in roasting pan.
4. Roast uncovered at 325°F 3 hours. Remove fat from pan as it accumulates during this period. Turn goose breast side up. Roast 1 to 2 hours longer, or until goose tests done. To test for doneness, move leg gently by grasping end of bone; drumstick-thigh joint should move easily. (Protect fingers with paper napkin.) Allow about 25 minutes per pound to estimate total roasting time.
5. To serve, remove skewers and cord. Place goose on heated platter. Remove some of the apples from goose and arrange on the platter. Garnish with the reserved prunes. For an attractive garnish, place cooked prunes on top of cooked apple rings, if desired.

Roast Goose with Sauerkraut Stuffing

ABOUT
8 SERVINGS

1 goose (ready-to-cook 10 to
    12 pounds)
1 tablespoon butter or
    margarine
2 large onions, chopped
6½ cups drained sauerkraut,
    snipped
2 medium apples, quartered,
    cored, and diced
1 small carrot, pared and
    shredded
2 medium potatoes, shredded
    (about 1½ cups)
½ cup dry white wine
1 to 2 tablespoons brown
    sugar
2 teaspoons caraway seed
½ teaspoon seasoned pepper
Salt

1. Singe and clean goose removing any large layers of fat from the body and neck cavities. Rinse thoroughly, drain, and pat dry with absorbent paper; set aside.
2. Heat butter in a skillet; add onion and cook until crisp-tender, 3 to 5 minutes.
3. Meanwhile, combine kraut, apple, carrot, and potato in a large bowl; toss until mixed. Add the onion, wine, and a blend of brown sugar, caraway seed, and seasoned pepper; toss again.
4. Rub cavities of goose with salt; lightly spoon stuffing into the body and neck cavities. Truss goose; set, breast side up, on a rack in a shallow roasting pan.
5. Roast, uncovered, in a 325°F oven about 3½ hours, or until goose tests done. Remove stuffing to a serving dish and accompany with slices of the roast goose.

Squabs, Pigeons, and Game Birds

Squabs en Casserole

SERVES 6

6 squabs, cleaned and
  drawn
Salt and pepper
1 sprig parsley
1 small carrot, diced
1 small onion, sliced
1 bay leaf
1 cup chicken stock
1 tablespoon butter or
  other fat
1 tablespoon flour
12 mushrooms, sautéed
1 tablespoon tomato
  catchup
2 tablespoons sherry

1. Season squabs with salt and pepper.
2. Stuff if desired.
3. Place in casserole with parsley, carrot, onion, bay leaf and chicken stock.
4. Cover and bake in moderate oven (350°F.) until tender, about 1 hour.
5. Remove squabs from liquid.
6. Melt fat, add flour and blend; add liquid from casserole and cook until thickened, stirring constantly.
7. Add mushrooms, catchup and sherry.
8. Replace squabs in casserole, pour sauce over them.

Note: If desired, add vegetables such as asparagus, broccoli or potatoes.

Squab and Mushroom Stew

SERVES 6

3 plumb squabs
3 tablespoons fat
2 cups stock or gravy
2 tablespoons tomato
  catchup
Salt and pepper to season
Cayenne
1 8-oz. can mushrooms,
  drained
2 tablespoons cream

1. Clean and singe squabs; cut into serving portions and cook slowly in fat; do not brown.
2. Add stock, catchup, salt, pepper and cayenne.
3. Simmer for 2 hours or until tender, add mushrooms and cook for 10 minutes longer, then stir in cream.
4. Arrange the mushrooms around squabs on a hot platter.

Squabs on Toast

SERVES 6

6 plump squabs
4 cups sage stuffing
3 slices bacon
1 carrot
1 onion, diced
1 teaspoon minced parsley
4 cups hot water or stock
¼ cup fat
¼ cup flour
6 slices buttered toast

1. Clean and dress squabs; stuff, truss and place them upright in a saucepan on slices of bacon.
2. Add carrot, onion and parsley and cover with water or stock.
3. Cover pan and simmer for 2 to 3 hours or until tender.
4. Melt fat, blend in flour and add 2 cups of the stock in which squabs were cooked.
5. Cook until thick, stirring constantly.
6. Serve each squab on a piece of toast and pour gravy over all.

Smothered Pigeons

2 SERVINGS

3 tablespoons butter
2 pigeons (about 2 pounds)
3 onions, sliced
1 cup meat stock or broth
2 tart apples, cored and sliced
¼ cup sliced mushrooms
Juice of ½ lemon
⅓ cup Madeira
1 tablespoon butter or margarine (at room temperature)
1 tablespoon Browned Flour
1 cup sour cream

1. Melt butter in a large skillet. Sauté pigeons in butter 15 minutes. Remove pigeons.
2. Fry onions in the butter left in skillet until tender. Add stock, sliced apples, mushrooms, and lemon juice. Mix well and bring to boiling. Add wine.
3. Mix butter with flour until smooth. Stir into liquid in skillet. Cook and stir until mixture is thickened.
4. Dip pigeons in sour cream; return to skillet. Cook, covered, until tender.

Browned Flour: Spread **1½ cups all-purpose flour** in a shallow baking pan. Place on lowest position for broiler. Broil and stir about 20 minutes, or until flour is golden brown. Stirring must be almost constant to prevent burning. If flour burns, skim off burned portion and continue browning remainder. Store in tightly covered container.
ABOUT 1⅓ CUPS

Baked Pigeon

1 SERVING

1 pigeon
Salt and pepper
1 strip bacon, diced
Melted butter

1. Soak the pigeon about 2 hours in cold water. Dry with paper towels.
2. Sprinkle cavity with salt and pepper.
3. Make small slits in skin; insert pieces of bacon. Place in a roasting pan.
4. Bake at 350°F 30 to 40 minutes, or until tender; baste often with butter.

Barbecued Wild Game Birds

4 SERVINGS

4 ready-to-cook wild game birds such as duckling, snipe, teal, or woodcock
Amber rum
6 peppercorns
4 parsley sprigs
3 garlic cloves
1 green hot pepper
1 tablespoon salt
1 tablespoon olive or peanut oil
1 cup red wine
Bacon drippings
Dry bread crumbs
Creole Barbecue Sauce (page 74)

1. Brush surface of birds with rum. Split birds in half and pound with a meat hammer.
2. In a mortar, pound to a paste the peppercorns, parsley, garlic, pepper, and salt. Mix seasoning paste with olive oil and wine. Pour marinade over birds and refrigerate 12 hours.
3. Thoroughly drain bird halves. Brush with bacon drippings and coat with bread crumbs.
4. Barbecue bird halves in a hinged grill 4 inches from glowing coals about 10 minutes on each side, basting twice with Creole Barbecue Sauce; time depends on their size. Turn birds once and baste again.
5. Birds should be eaten on the rare side; when birds are pricked with a fork, a droplet of blood should surface slowly.

Roast Guinea Hen

SERVES 4 TO 6

2 2-pound guinea hens
Stuffing
¼ pound salt pork, thinly
  sliced
3 tablespoons butter,
  melted

1. Clean and rinse hens. Pat dry.
2. Fill cavities with stuffing; truss birds.
3. Place on rack in shallow pan, breast side down.
4. Cover with salt pork.
5. Roast at 350°F. for 1 hour.
6. Remove from oven.
7. Discard salt pork and turn breast up.
8. Brush birds with butter and continue roasting until tender, about 30 to 45 minutes.

Guinea Stew

2 SERVINGS

Salt and freshly ground
  pepper
1 guinea fowl (2½ to 3
  pounds)
1 lime, halved
¼ pound salt pork, cubed
4 parsley sprigs
2 scallions or green onions,
  chopped
2 garlic cloves
2 cloves
½ teaspoon salt
¼ cup soybean oil
½ cup amber rum
2 cups red wine
1 cup chicken stock
12 shallots
2 carrots, sliced
2 turnips, sliced
1 tablespoon butter
1 tablespoon cornstarch

1. Sprinkle salt, and pepper over bird and refrigerate overnight. The next day, rub the skin with the cut side of the lime. Cut bird into pieces.
2. Render salt pork over medium heat in a Dutch oven. When crisp, remove the cracklings.
3. In a mortar, pound to a paste the parsley, scallions, garlic, cloves, and salt. Add the seasoning paste and oil to the Dutch oven.
4. Sauté the meat until golden brown on all sides.
5. Heat rum, ignite it, and pour it, still flaming, over the meat. Add wine and stock; reduce heat, cover, and simmer 30 minutes.
6. Add shallots, carrots, and turnips. Simmer until meat and vegetables are tender.
7. Place meat and vegetables on a serving platter.
8. Mix butter and cornstarch; add to liquid in Dutch oven and stir over high heat until sauce is slightly thickened. Season with salt and pepper, if necessary. Pour sauce over meat and vegetables.
9. Serve with Caribbean Rice (page 77).

Chicken Stew: Follow recipe for Guinea Stew, substituting **1 broiler-fryer chicken (about 2 pounds)** for guinea fowl.

Quail Baked in Wine

ABOUT 1 QUAIL PER PERSON

½ cup fat
2 small onions, minced
2 whole cloves
1 teaspoon peppercorns
2 cloves garlic, cut fine
½ bay leaf
6 quail, cleaned and trussed
2 cups white wine
½ teaspoon salt
⅛ teaspoon pepper
Few grains cayenne
1 teaspoon minced chives
2 cups cream or evaporated
  milk

1. Melt fat, add onions, cloves, peppercorns, garlic and bay leaf; cook for several minutes.
2. Add quail and brown on all sides.
3. Add wine, salt, pepper, cayenne and chives and simmer until tender, about 30 minutes.
4. Remove quail to hot serving dish.
5. Strain sauce, add cream and heat to boiling point.
6. Pour over quail.

Teal on the Spit

4 SERVINGS

4 teals; reserve livers
1 orange, halved
8 chicken livers
1 tablespoon flour
¼ teaspoon garlic powder
Salt and pepper
2 tablespoons olive oil
4 bacon slices
2 tablespoons flour
2 tablespoons butter
1 can (13 ounces) clear consommé madrilène
1½ teaspoons lime juice
1½ teaspoons orange juice

1. Rub teals with cut sides of orange halves. Set aside.
2. Coat the teal livers and chicken livers with a mixture of 1 tablespoon flour, garlic powder, salt, and pepper. Heat oil and sauté the livers until golden brown.
3. Put the livers into the bird cavities. Wrap each bird in a slice of bacon, securing with skewers.
4. Spear birds on a spit and broil on the electric broiler about 25 minutes or, if charcoal is used, place the spitted bird 4 inches from the hot coals and turn often.
5. Brown 2 tablespoons flour in butter in a small saucepan over high heat. Add enough consommé madrilène to just moisten the mixture, stirring rapidly with a whisk. While it thickens, slowly pour in the remaining consommé in a thin stream. Boil rapidly, uncovered, stirring constantly for about 4 minutes, or until the sauce is reduced to ½ cup. Remove from heat and add lime juice and orange juice.
6. Serve teal with Stuffed Tomatoes with Rice and Pine Nuts (page 76) and the sauce separately.

Ortolans on Croutons

8 SERVINGS

8 ortolans
½ lime
Salt and freshly ground
    pepper
½ cup cubed salt pork
¼ cup amber rum
½ cup red wine
1 tablespoon butter
1 tablespoon cornstarch
8 white bread slices with
    crusts trimmed
¼ cup butter

1. Truss ortolans. Rub the skin with the cut side of the lime half. Season with salt and pepper.
2. Render the salt pork over high heat in a Dutch oven. Sauté ortolans for 6 minutes, or until well browned.
3. Heat rum, ignite it, and pour it, still flaming, over the birds. Place birds on a serving platter.
4. Pour wine into Dutch oven to deglaze. Mix 1 tablespoon butter and cornstarch and add to wine. Stir until sauce is slightly thicker.
5. Make croutons by frying bread slices in butter until brown on both sides.
6. Serve each ortolan on a crouton, top with a slice of sautéed liver pâté, if desired, and pour sauce over all.

Wild Duck, Goose, or Partridge

4 SERVINGS

2 partridges, 1 duck, or 1
    goose
12 peppercorns
1 onion, quartered
Salt
14 to 20 juniper seeds,
    ground or mashed
2 tablespoons bacon drip-
    pings or butter
½ cup water
2 cups sliced red cabbage
1 large onion, sliced
½ cup water
1 tablespoon cornstarch or
    potato starch
2 tablespoons water
½ teaspoon sugar
1 teaspoon vinegar
¾ cup red wine

1. Place partridges in a plastic bag with peppercorns and quartered onion. Refrigerate 3 days to age.
2. Discard peppercorns and quartered onion. Cut up bird. Sprinkle with salt and juniper. Let stand 1 hour.
3. Heat bacon drippings in a large skillet. Brown bird in the drippings; add ½ cup water. Cover and simmer 1 hour.
4. Add cabbage, sliced onion, and ½ cup water. Cover and simmer 30 minutes. Remove the meat to a warmed platter.
5. Mix the cornstarch with 2 tablespoons water to make a smooth paste. Stir into drippings in pan.
6. Stir in sugar and vinegar; bring to boiling. Cook and stir 2 minutes. Remove from heat. Stir in wine.

Pot-Roasted Wild Duck

8 SERVINGS

4 wild ducks (about 2
   pounds each)
Amber rum
8 limes, peeled
8 peppercorns, cracked
Papaya leaves
Bacon drippings
3 tablespoons soybean oil
12 shallots
⅓ cup amber rum
½ cup stock
1 carrot
1 garlic clove, crushed in a
   garlic press
1 thyme sprig
1 parsley sprig
1 green hot pepper
2 cups hot stock
2 tablespoons butter
2 tablespoons cornstarch
Salt and pepper to taste
8 slices bread, toasted
¼ cup butter

1. Wipe the duck with rum. Place 2 limes and 2 peppercorns in the cavity of each duck. Wrap the birds in papaya leaves to tenderize and refrigerate 12 hours.
2. Brush bacon drippings on each bird. Heat the oil in a Dutch oven and sauté ducks and shallots until the birds are brown on all sides.
3. Heat rum, ignite it, and pour it, while still flaming, over the birds. Add the ½ cup stock, carrot, garlic, thyme, parsley, and hot pepper. Cover Dutch oven.
4. Cook in a 475°F oven 30 minutes.
5. Cut the breasts in one piece and slice off remaining meat; reserve. Discard limes and peppercorns.
6. In a mortar, pound the carcasses until broken up. Pour the hot stock into the Dutch oven; add the broken carcasses and boil 10 minutes. Remove the hot pepper. Strain the stock and return to the Dutch oven.
7. Mix butter and cornstarch. Add to the stock; stir over medium heat until slightly thickened. Add salt and pepper to taste.
8. Fry toasted bread in butter until golden and crisp. Arrange meat on croutons. Pour sauce over all.
9. Garnish with Stuffed Sweet Peppers (page 77).   Serve remaining sauce from a sauceboat.

Wild Duck Pâté

2 wild ducks (about 4
   pounds each); reserve livers
¼ cup olive oil
Juice of 2 limes
1 garlic clove, halved
Water
1 carrot
1 leek
1 teaspoon salt
⅛ teaspoon pepper
1 cup port wine
2 bay leaves
1 small onion, minced
1 green hot pepper
⅛ teaspoon thyme
3 tablespoons olive oil
3 tablespoons butter
½ pound beef liver, cubed
¼ cup amber rum
1 egg
Lard
Truffles (optional)
Bay leaves and green hot
   peppers for garnish

1. Marinate the ducks for ½ hour in a mixture of ¼ cup oil and lime juice. Rub ducks with the cut surface of garlic clove.
2. Place birds in a Dutch oven and cover with water; add carrot, leek, salt, and pepper and bring to a boil. Simmer covered over low heat until birds are tender.
3. Remove birds from broth and cool. Reserve ¼ cup broth; store remaining broth for future use. Remove the meat from the carcasses, cutting the breast meat into long, even strips.
4. Mix port wine, bay leaves, onion, pepper, and thyme; marinate the breast meat for ½ hour. Set aside remaining duck meat.
5. Heat 3 tablespoons oil and butter in a medium skillet. Sauté duck livers and beef liver over high heat until golden. Warm the rum, ignite it, and pour it, still flaming, over the livers. Stir in ¼ cup of the reserved broth to deglaze the skillet.
6. Purée in an electric blender the liver mixture, reserved duck meat, and egg.
7. Coat heavily with lard 1 large terrine or loaf dish, or 2 small terrines or loaf dishes. Put in half the puréed mixture, then arrange the marinated strips of duck breast on top with slices of truffles, if desired. Cover with the remaining duck mixture, then with a thick coat of lard.

(continued)

8. Garnish with bay leaves and green hot peppers. Cover terrine and place in a pan of hot water.
9. Bake at 375°F about 1½ hours.
10. Wipe clean the sides of the terrine. Cool and store covered in refrigerator up to a week.
11. To serve, remove bay leaves and peppers; slice pâté and accompany with salad.

Pheasant

4 SERVINGS

1 Pheasant
1 to 1½ teaspoons salt
½ teaspoon black pepper
8 medium peeled raw potatoes
1 to 1½ teaspoons salt
3 tablespoons butter
¾ cup heavy cream
1 ounce apple cheese
2 teaspoon soy sauce
1 large bunch parsley sprigs

1. Rinse and wipe the pheasant inside and outside. Season with salt and pepper, half inside and half outside. Brown the pheasant quickly all around in a frying pan in half the butter. Wrap in aluminum foil.
2. Preheat the oven to 325°F.
3. Cut the peeled raw potatoes in slices and fry them lightly on both sides in the remaining butter in the pan. Later add the rest of the butter. Sprinkle some salt over each round of potato slices before they are transferred to an ovenproof deep dish or casserole.
4. Distribute the potato slices evenly on the bottom and up towards the edge of the casserole, place the pheasant in the middle and pour on the gravy from foil if there is any.
5. Cover the casserole immediately. Put the casserole in the oven and roast the pheasant for about 30 minutes.
6. Whip together cream, apple cheese and soy sauce. Taste and correct seasoning, adding more apple cheese if necessary.
7. Pour the cream mixture on pheasant and potatoes when the casserole has been in the oven for 20 minutes. Serve dish straight from the oven with the pheasant cut in four portion sizes, and garnish with fresh parsley sprigs.

Potted Pheasant

2 TO 4 SERVINGS

¾ cup all-purpose flour
½ teaspoon salt
¼ teaspoon pepper
1 pheasant, cut in pieces
½ cup butter
1 onion, quartered
1 stalk celery, cut up
2 cups meat stock or beef broth
3 whole allspice
½ cup whipping cream
2 tablespoons sherry

1. Mix flour with salt and pepper.
2. Coat each piece of pheasant with seasoned flour. Melt butter in a Dutch oven or flameproof casserole. Brown pheasant in butter. Add onion, celery, and 1 cup meat stock. Cover.
3. Bake at 350°F 40 minutes. Add remaining meat stock. Do not cover. Bake about 40 minutes longer, or until pheasant is tender.
4. Remove pheasant to heated platter. Strain broth; combine 1 cup broth to cream and sherry. Serve over the pheasant.

Pheasant

Sauces and Side Dishes

Chicken Stock

3 TO 3½
QUARTS

5 pounds chicken backs and
  wings, or stewing chicken,
  cut up
3 carrots, cut in 2-inch
  pieces
2 medium yellow onions,
  quartered
1 stalk celery, cut in 2-inch
  pieces
2 teaspoons salt
Bouquet garni:
  ¾ teaspoon dried thyme
    leaves
  ¾ teaspoon dried rosemary
    leaves
  1 bay leaf
  4 sprigs parsley
  2 whole cloves
Water

1. Place chicken, vegetables, salt, and bouquet garni in an 8-quart Dutch oven. Pour in water to cover (about 4 quarts). Simmer covered 2 to 2½ hours.
2. Strain stock through a double thickness of cheesecloth into a storage container. Taste for seasoning. If more concentrated flavor is desired, return stock to saucepan and simmer 20 to 30 minutes, or dissolve 1 to 2 teaspoons instant chicken bouillon in the stock.
3. Store covered in refrigerator or freezer. Remove solidified fat from top of stock before using.

Note: Refrigerated stock is perishable. If not used within several days, heat to boiling, cool, and refrigerate or freeze to prevent spoilage. Stock can be kept frozen up to 4 months.

Creole Barbecue Sauce

ABOUT
3½ CUPS

1 can (28 ounces) Italian
  plum tomatoes, drained
1 medium onion, finely
  chopped
⅔ cup olive oil
2 garlic cloves, crushed in a
  garlic press
¼ cup lime juice
1 teaspoon salt
⅛ teaspoon dried basil
Dash pepper
Bouquet garni
5 drops Tabasco

1. Chop tomatoes; put tomato and onion into a saucepan and cook uncovered over medium heat for 15 minutes.
2. Force tomato mixture through a fine sieve into another saucepan. Discard remaining solids.
3. Add remaining ingredients to saucepan. Stir until blended. Simmer uncovered about 1 hour, stirring occasionally.
4. Brush sauce over meat for barbecuing.

Giblet Gravy

3 CUPS GRAVY

Chicken liver, heart and
  gizzard
¼ cup chicken fat
¼ cup flour
 3 cups giblet stock*

1. Cook giblets and finely chop.
2. Melt fat; add flour and brown lightly, stirring constantly.
3. Add giblet stock, stirring constantly.
4. Cook about 5 minutes, or until thick.
5. Add the giblets and season.

* Cream or milk may be used for part of the stock.

Tomato Sauce Creole

⅓ cup peanut oil
2 medium onions, thinly
  sliced
6 Italian plum tomatoes,
  peeled, seeded, and finely
  chopped
½ cup beef stock
Salt and freshly ground pepper to taste
3 drops Tabasco
1 garlic clove, crushed in a
  garlic press

1. Heat oil in a saucepan, add onion, and cook over low heat until translucent but not browned. Add tomato, stock, and seasonings; stir with a wooden spoon until tomato pulp is cooked to a fine purée.
2. Serve with rice or grilled meats.

Green Peppercorn Sauce

ABOUT
2½ CUPS

1 cup Chicken Stock (page
  74)
2 tablespoons brandy
1 tablespoon arrowroot
Cold water
¼ pound fresh mushrooms,
  chopped
¼ cup Mock Crème Fraîche
  (page 76)
½ teaspoon salt
¼ teaspoon freshly ground
  pepper
2 tablespoons drained green
  peppercorns

1. Heat stock and brandy.
2. Mix arrowroot with a little cold water; stir into stock. Simmer, stirring constantly, until stock has thickened (about 4 minutes). Stir in remaining ingredients. Heat thoroughly. Serve immediately.

Madeira Sauce

ABOUT
1½ CUPS

1 cup Chicken Stock (page
  74)
Juice of 1 lemon
1 teaspoon Worcestershire
  sauce
¼ teaspoon salt
⅓ cup Madeira wine
1 tablespoon arrowroot
Cold water
1 tablespoon snipped parsley

1. Heat stock, lemon juice, Worcestershire sauce, salt, and Madeira in a small saucepan.
2. Mix arrowroot with a little cold water; stir into stock mixture. Simmer, stirring constantly, until thickened (about 3 minutes). Stir in parsley. Serve immediately.

Cumberland Sauce

ABOUT
1½ CUPS

½ cup fresh cranberries
2 teaspoons grated orange
  peel
1 large navel orange, peeled
  and finely chopped
2 tablespoons brandy
½ cup port wine
¼ cup orange juice
¼ cup Beef Stock
1 teaspoon prepared mustard

1. Process cranberries, orange peel and chopped orange, and brandy in a food processor or blender until finely ground.
2. Transfer mixture to a saucepan; stir in remaining ingredients. Simmer uncovered until sauce is of medium thick consistency (about 15 minutes). Serve hot, or refrigerate and serve cold.
3. Serve over duck, pork, ham, or over cottage cheese or fruit salads.

Mock Crème Fraîche

ABOUT
2 CUPS

1½ cups Neufchatel cheese
6 tablespoons Low-Fat
Yogurt (below)

1. Mix cheese and yogurt in a blender or food processor until smooth and fluffy. Place in small jars; cover tightly.
2. Set jars in a warm place (100° to 125°F) for 2 hours; see Note. Cool and refrigerate. Stir before using.

Note: Use an oven thermometer in making Mock Crème Fraîche, as temperature is very important. A gas oven with a pilot light will be about 125°F. Turn electric oven to as warm a setting as necessary to maintain temperature. Mock Crème Fraîche can be refrigerated up to 3 weeks.

Low-Fat Yogurt

ABOUT
1 QUART

1 quart 2% milk
¼ cup instant nonfat
dry-milk
2 tablespoons low-fat natural
yogurt

1. Mix milk and dry-milk solids in a medium saucepan. Heat to scalding (150°F); cool to 110°F. Stir in yogurt.
2. Transfer mixture to a glass or crockery bowl. Cover with plastic wrap; wrap bowl securely in a heavy bath towel. Set in warm place (100° to 125°F)* for 4 to 6 hours, until yogurt has formed.
3. Place several layers of paper toweling directly on yogurt; refrigerate covered until cold.

*A gas oven with a pilot light will be about 125°F; however, use an oven thermometer, as temperature is very important. Turn an electric oven to as warm a setting as necessary to maintain temperature.
   Excess liquid and a coarse texture will result if temperature is too high. Liquid can be drained with a nylon baster. Blend yogurt in a food processor or blender to restore texture.

Note: This recipe can be made using skim or reconstituted dry milk, although the product will not be as rich.
   Purchased low-fat natural yogurt can be substituted in any recipe.

Stuffed Tomatoes with Rice and Pine Nuts

6 SERVINGS

8 large firm tomatoes with
tops sliced off and reserved
Salt, pepper, and sugar to
taste
¾ cup olive oil
4 onions, minced
1 cup long-grain rice
½ cup water
½ cup chopped parsley
½ cup dried currants
½ cup pine nuts
1 teaspoon mint
Juice of 1 lemon
2 cups water

1. Scoop out pulp from tomatoes and reserve. Sprinkle insides of tomatoes with salt, pepper, and sugar. Arrange in a baking dish.
2. Heat ¼ cup oil in a large skillet. Add onion, pulp, rice, water, parsley, currants, pine nuts, mint, and lemon juice. Simmer, covered, stirring occasionally, until liquid is absorbed. Cool slightly. Adjust seasonings.
3. Fill tomatoes with rice mixture. Replace tops and put into baking dish. Drizzle remaining olive oil between tomatoes. Add water.
4. Bake at 350°F about 40 minutes, or until rice is cooked; baste occasionally. If necessary, add a little water. Serve hot or chilled.

Stuffed Sweet Peppers

4 SERVINGS

4 red or green sweet
  peppers, halved lengthwise
Stock
1 cup cooked rice
2 cups cooked ground beef,
  ham, or poultry
Shredded cheese
Tomato Sauce Creole
  (page 75)

1. Parboil pepper halves in stock to cover. Drain peppers and reserve stock.
2. Mix rice and meat; stuff peppers. Sprinkle tops with cheese. Arrange peppers in a baking dish; add reserved stock to dish.
3. Bake at 350°F 30 minutes, or until well browned. Serve in the baking dish and accompany with the sauce.

Dinner Crêpes

ABOUT
18 CREPES

1 cup all-purpose flour
⅛ teaspoon salt
3 eggs
1½ cups milk
2 tablespoons melted butter
  or oil

1. Sift flour and salt. Add eggs, one at a time, beating thoroughly. Gradually add milk, mixing until blended. Add melted butter or oil and beat until smooth. (Or mix in an electric blender until smooth.)
2. Let batter stand for 1 hour before cooking crepes.

Tube Method: Place filling in a line down the center of the crepe. Lift edge and tuck under filling. Roll up firmly.

Caribbean Rice

8 SERVINGS

4 parsley sprigs
3 peppercorns
2 garlic cloves
2 scallions or green onions,
  cut in pieces
1½ teaspoons salt
½ teaspoon thyme
2 tablespoons peanut oil
2 cups rice
4½ cups chicken broth
1 bay leaf
1 green hot pepper or ½
  teaspoon cayenne or red
  pepper

1. In a mortar, pound parsley, peppercorns, garlic, scallions, salt, and thyme to a paste. Set aside.
2. Heat oil in a large, heavy saucepan; add rice. Stir until all the rice is coated with oil and turns chalky.
3. Add seasoning paste and chicken broth; bring to a boil. Reduce heat and add bay leaf and pepper. Cover saucepan and cook undisturbed for 20 minutes.
4. Remove the cover; continue to cook over low heat for 5 minutes, or until no liquid remains.
5. Discard bay leaf and whole pepper. Fluff rice and serve.

Rice and Avocado: Follow recipe for Caribbean Rice. Place **cubed avocado** on top of the rice for the last 5 minutes of cooking. Mix in avocado when rice is fluffed.

Coconut and Rice: Follow recipe for Caribbean Rice, using **brown rice** and an additional **½ cup chicken broth**. Add **1 cup freshly grated coconut** along with bay leaf and pepper. Proceed as directed.

Saffron Rice: Steep **½ teaspoon Spanish saffron** in **2¼ cups boiling water** until it turns bright orange. Strain. Follow recipe for Caribbean Rice, using saffron water in place of some of the chicken broth to cook the rice.

Smothered Mixed Vegetables

8 small carrots, sliced
8 small potatoes
4 medium white turnips, pared and sliced
4 medium tomatoes, peeled, seeded, and quartered
2 small chayote or zucchini, sliced
1 green and 1 red sweet pepper, cut in strips
1 small eggplant (unpeeled), diced
Cauliflower chunks
½ cup green peas
½ cup lima beans
2 tablespoons peanut oil
1 large Spanish onion, sliced
1 cup stock or beef broth
¼ cup peanut oil
1 tablespoon salt
Freshly ground pepper
1 garlic clove, crushed in a garlic press
4 dried Italian pepper pods or 1 pink hot pepper
1 tablespoon tomato paste

1. Arrange in a top-of-range casserole with lid the sliced carrot, potatoes, turnip slices, tomato quarters, sliced chayote, pepper strips, diced eggplant, cauliflower chunks, peas, and beans.
2. Heat 2 tablespoons oil in a skillet over medium heat. Add onion and sauté until golden. Add stock, ¼ cup oil, salt, pepper, and garlic; pour over vegetables in casserole. Lay pepper pods over vegetables; cover and cook covered over low heat 45 minutes.
3. Remove cover, increase heat, and cook off most of the liquid. Remove peppers and stir tomato paste into vegetable mixture.

Bananas à l'Antillaise

6 green-tipped bananas, peeled and halved
2 cups dry white wine
Salt to taste
2 tablespoons butter
2 tablespoons flour
⅛ teaspoon mace
⅛ teaspoon cloves
Cayenne or red pepper to taste

1. Put bananas into a saucepan with wine and salt. Bring to a boil, cover, and simmer 25 minutes.
2. Blend butter, flour, mace, cloves, and pepper.
3. Remove fruit from saucepan. Stir butter mixture into liquid in saucepan. Boil and stir 3 minutes.
4. Serve the fruit and sauce in a dish as an accompaniment to roast pork.

Index

Arroz con Pollo, 18

Baked Pigeon, 68
Bananas à l'Antillaise, 78
Barbecued Chicken, Quail or
    Guinea Fowl, 16
Barbecued Wild Game
    Birds, 68
Barbecue Sauce, Creole, 74
Basil Dumplings, 23
Basque Chicken with
    Olives, 21
Bouillon Cocq, 23
Braised Chicken and
    Onions, 26
Bread Stuffing, 11
Breast of Chicken
    Savannah, 30
Broiled Chicken, 14
Broiled Chicken in Lemon
    Juice and Oregano, 15
Broiled Chicken with
    Tomatoes, 14
Broiled Marinated Chicken, 15
Browned Flour, 68
Brunswick Stew, 22

Canard à l'Orange, 64
Capon
    in Cream, 30
    Roasted in Salt, 11
    Roast Stuffed, 11
Casserole
    Chicken and Tomato, 31
    Chicken Artichoke, 31
    Chicken-Green Noodle, 32
Caribbean Rice, 77
Chicken
    à la King, 24
    and Asparagus Salad, 46
    and Bacon Salad, 46
    and Cabbage Salad, 46
    and Chestnut Salad, 46
    and Cucumber Salad, 46
    and Dumplings, 23
    and Onions, Braised, 26
    and Orange Salad, 46
    and Rice Valencia, 39
    and Tomato Casserole, 31
    and Tongue Salad, 47

and Vegetables, Skillet, 28
and Wild Rice, 34
Artichoke Casserole, 31
Bake, Swiss, 41
Breasts
    Regina, 17
    with Sour Cream, 38
    with Yogurt Sauce, 26
Broiled, 14
Cacciatore, 21
-Cheese Pies, 42
Chili Casserole,
    Mexican, 32
-Chip Bake, 41
Country Style, 18
Curry with Rice, 30
Easy Oriental Style, 36
en Cocotte, 36
Flavor-Full Broiled, 14
French-Fried, 16
Fried, 16
Fried, Crunchy, 16
Green, 29
-Green Noodle
    Casserole, 32
Halves, Country-
    Flavored, 34
Honey-Glazed Filbert
    Roast, 9
in Filo, 45
in Lemon Juice and
    Oregano, Broiled, 15
Italiano, 42
Kentucky Fried, 16
Livers and Mushrooms, 47
Livers in Madeira Sauce, 47
Mac, 39
Marengo, 24
Martinique Stuffed in
    Rum, 13
Mexicana, 28
Mousse Amandine, 45
Novaes, 38
or Turkey Mole Poblano, 44
Oven-Fried, Oriental, 17
Pie, 42
Pie, Old-Fashioned, 44
Piquant, 31
Polish Style, 34
Quail, or Guinea Fowl,
    Barbecued, 16
Roast
    Pennsylvania Dutch, 11
    Tarragon, 10
    with Orange-Beer
        Sauce, 9
    with Potatoes, 9
Royal, 26
Salad, 46

Salad Mold, Dubonnet, 46
Savannah, Breast of, 30
Spiced Fruited, 77
Stew, 69
Stock, 74
Stuffed, Jamaican Style, 13
Surprise, 32
Sweet and Sour, 27
Tablecloth Stainer, 22
Tetrazzini, 41
Vesuvio, 39
with Cheese, 24
with Curried Fruit,
    Crispy, 36
with Ham, 34
with Mushrooms, Herb, 38
with Olives, Basque, 21
with Poached Garlic, 12
with Rice, 18
with Tomatoes, Broiled, 14
Coconut and Rice, 77
Cooked Giblets and Broth, 57
Cornish Hens
    Spit-Roasted, 49
    with Raisin Stuffing, 49
Country-Flavored Chicken
    Halves, 34
Country Style Chicken, 18
Crème Fraîche, Mock, 76
Creole Barbecue Sauce, 74
Crêpes, Dinner, 77
Crispy Chicken with Curried
    Fruit, 36
Crumb-Crusted Duckling
    Halves, 60
Crunchy Fried Chicken, 16
Cumberland Sauce, 75
Curried Duck Martinique, 61
Curried Fruit, 37

Dinner Crêpes, 77
Dubonnet Chicken Salad
    Mold, 46
Duckling
    Bigarade, 60
    Goose or Partridge, Wild, 70
    Gourmet, Glazed, 62
    Halves, Crumb-Crusted, 60
    in Caper Sauce,
        Smothered, 59
    Martinique, Curried, 61
    Pâté, 71
    Pot-Roasted Wild, 71
    with Fruit Salad, 61
    with Green Peppercorn
        Sauce, 59
    with Olives, Roast, 62
    with Red Cabbage, 59
Dumplings, Basil, 23

Flavor-Full Broiled
    Chicken, 14
Flour, Browned, 68
French-Fried Chicken, 16
Fried Chicken, 16

Game Birds, Barbecued
    Wild, 68
Game Hens with Spicy
    Stuffing, 48
Giblets
    and Broth, Cooked, 57
    Gravy, 74
    with Rice, 47
Glazed Duckling Gourmet, 62
Goose
    with Prune-Apple Stuffing,
        Roast, 66
    with Rice-and-Pickle
        Stuffing, Roast, 65
    with Sauerkraut Stuffing,
        Roast, 66
Green Chicken, 29
Green Peppercorn Sauce, 75
Guinea Hen, Roast, 69
Guinea Stew, 69

Hens in Wine, 48
Herb Bouquet, 24
Herb Butters, 14
Herb-Chicken with
    Mushrooms, 38
Honey-Glazed Filbert Roast
    Chicken, 9

Kentucky Fried Chicken, 16

Low-Fat Yogurt, 76

Madeira Sauce, 75
Marinated Chicken,
    Broiled, 15
Martinique Stuffed Chicken in
    Rum, 13
Mexican Chili Chicken
    Casserole, 32
Mixed Vegetables,
    Smothered, 78
Mock Crème Fraîche, 76

Old-Fashioned Chicken
    Pie, 44
Oriental Oven-Fried
    Chicken, 17
Ortolans on Croutons, 70
Oyster Stuffing, 52

Pennsylvania Dutch Roast
    Chicken, 11

Peppercorn Sauce, Green, 75
Pheasant, Potted, 72
Pie, Chicken, 42
Pies, Chicken-Cheese, 42
Pigeon
 Baked, 68
 Smothered, 68
Piquant Chicken, 31
Pot-Roasted Wild Duck, 71
Potted Pheasant, 72

Quail Baked in Wine, 69

Rice
 and Avocado, 77
 Caribbean, 77
 Saffron, 77
Roast
 Capon, Stuffed, 11
 Chicken Tarragon, 10
 Chicken with Orange-Beer
  Sauce, 9
 Chicken with Potatoes, 9
 Duckling with Olives, 62
 Goose with Prune-Apple
  Stuffing, 66
 Goose with Rice-and-Pickle
  Stuffing, 65
 Goose with Sauerkraut
  Stuffing, 66

Guinea Hen, 69
Half Turkey, 52
Rock Cornish Hen with Wild
  Rice and Mushrooms, 50
Stuffed Turkey, 54
Turkey I, II, III, 51, 52, 53
Turkey with Anchovies, 53
Turkey with Herbed
  Stuffing, 56
Turkey with
  Pineapple-Stuffed
  Breast, 57
Rock Cornish Hen(s), see also
  Cornish Hens, Hens, &
  Game Hens
 with Fruited Stuffing, 48
 with Oranges and
  Almonds, 50
 with Wild Rice and
  Mushrooms, Roast, 50
Royal Chicken, 26

Saffron Rice, 77
Salad, Chicken, 46, 47
Skillet Chicken and
  Vegetables, 28
Smothered
 Duck in Caper Sauce, 59
 Mixed Vegetables, 78
 Pigeon, 68

Spiced Fruited Chicken, 17
Spit-Roasted Cornish
  Hens, 49
Squab and Mushroom
  Stew, 67
Squabs en Casserole, 67
Squabs on Toast, 67
Stew
 Brunswick, 22
 Chicken, 69
 Guinea, 69
 Squab and Mushroom, 67
Stuffed
 Chicken, Jamaican
  Style, 13
 Roast Capon, 11
 Sweet Peppers, 77
 Tomatoes with Rice and
  Pine Nuts, 76
 Turkey, 54
Stuffing, 54
 Bread, 11
 for a Small Turkey, 56
 Oyster, 52
 Sweet Potato, 13
Sweet
  and Sour Chicken, 27
 Peppers, Stuffed, 77
 Potato Stuffing, 13
Swiss Chicken Bake, 41

Teal on the Spit, 70
Tomato Sauce Creole, 75
Turkey(s)
 Croquettes, 58
 'n' Dressing Bake, 58
 Pot Pie, 57
 Roast I, II, III, 51, 52, 53
 Roast Half, 52
 Roast Stuffed, 54
 Stuffed, 54
 with Anchovies, Roast, 53
 with Herbed Stuffing,
  Roast, 56
 with Pineapple-Stuffed
  Breast, Roast, 57
Tomatoes with Rice and Pine
  Nuts, Stuffed, 76

Wild
 Duck, Goose, or
  Partridge, 70
 Duck Pâté, 71
 Game Birds, Barbecued, 68

Yogurt, Low-Fat, 76